# Richard Tolson

# A SOLDIER POET

## Letters and Poems of an English Officer
## 1938 – 1952

© Rosalind Tolson 2009
*Richard Tolson ~ A Soldier Poet*

ISBN 978-0-9562246-0-6

Published by Tolson Publications
Flat 1
82 Banbury Road
Oxford
OX2 6JT

A CIP catalogue record of this book
can be obtained from the British Library.

Book designed by Michael Walsh at
THE BETTER BOOK COMPANY

Printed by
ASHFORD COLOUR PRESS
Unit 600 Fareham Reach
Fareham Road
Gosport
Hants PO13 0FW

# Acknowledgements

I would like to thank Anne Lorraine-Smith for making the original transcript of Richard's wartime diary, and James Kelly for typing the letters. I am grateful to Kate Easton, Cecily Drummond, Charles Foster, Janna deVere Green, Anne Hancock and Margaret Poston for encouragement and advice. I would also like to thank Colonel Robin McNish for military information; and Roderick Bailey for his interest, and for arranging the safe-keeping of Richard's letters and diary at the Imperial War Museum.

*for*
*William and Jane*

# CONTENTS

# POEMS

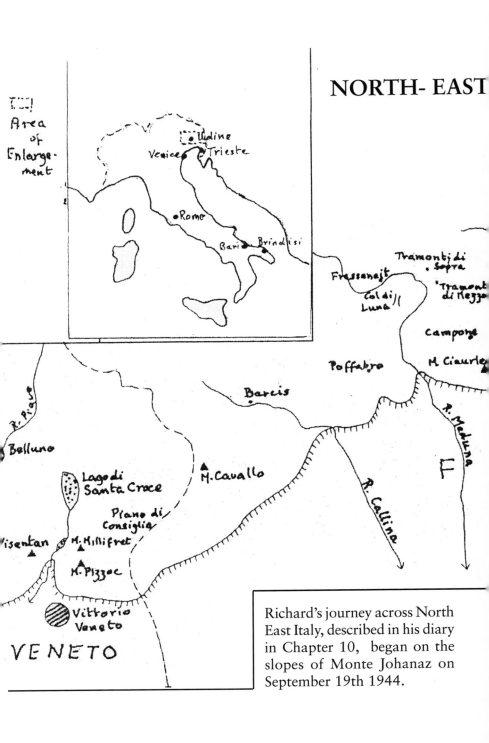

**NORTH- EAST**

Area of Enlargement

Udine
Venice • Trieste

Rome

Bari • Brindisi

Tramonti di Sopra

Frassenejt

Col di Luna

Tramont di Mezzo

Campone

Poffabro

M. Ciaurle

Barcis

R. Piave

R. Meduna

Belluno

R. Callina

F

M. Cavallo

Lago di Santa Croce

Piano di Consiglia

Visentan

M. Millifret

M. Pizzoc

Vittorio Veneto

VENETO

Richard's journey across North East Italy, described in his diary in Chapter 10, began on the slopes of Monte Johanaz on September 19th 1944.

He crossed the Tagliamento River near Trasaghis, and spent most of October and November in Tramonti di Sopra and Clauzetto. At the end of November, he and Tom Rowarth continued to Barcis where Tom remained, and Richard went on to the Piano di Consiglio to join Paul Breitsche.

*Back cover painting:*
*Covehithe:*
*a watercolour by Jamie Brice Lenkheit*

# Setting the Scene

Richard Tolson entered Sandhurst in August 1937. He joined the Royal Sussex Regiment in January 1939, and remained in the army until 1952 when he resigned. After his death in 2006, I found the letters he had written to his mother during his army career. There were also many poems, some of which I knew, but also many that I hadn't seen before. One of my friends described Richard as a "soldier poet", and in England at least there have been many of these. I found the letters very interesting, telling of many events he had talked about, but also others which were completely new to me. The style of writing changed, from that of a young man of 19, to that of the experienced soldier with a love of words, in his late twenties. Both the letters and the poetry give a view of an ordinary Officer's life for the years before, during and after World War II. I decided to collect the letters and the poetry into one volume.

The letters begin at Sandhurst in 1938. His first posting with the Royal Sussex early in 1939 was in Devonport. From there he moved to Belfast, and was in Belfast when war was declared on September 3rd. There were a few months training in England, before he was sent to France in April 1940 as part of the British Expeditionary Force. His Battalion, the 6th, escaped from France rather late, not via Dunkirk, but through St Nazaire.

Then followed three long years in England, in defence duties and in training. At last, in September 1943, he was posted to the Middle East. He spent some months running a Battle School in Palestine. But in 1944 he heard about an organisation called SOE (Special Operations Executive) which he joined in March. He was attached to Number 1 Special Force as a British liaison officer, and served with the Italian Partisans in North East Italy. SOE was set up in 1940 to give support to resistance movements, to help with sabotage and to distract the German army from front line duties. He was unable to write letters during this time, but he kept a diary, and I have included this in the chapters that follow.

When the war in Europe ended on May 8th, he had some leave before going to India, still with SOE. The war with Japan ended before he could be parachuted into the Celebes (now Sulawesi), but he stayed on in Bangkok until the end of 1946 with the psychological warfare department. His final years with the army were spent in the Middle East, Malta, Trieste and England.

Nearly all of Richard's letters were addressed to "Mummy". Richard's mother, Marjorie, was born in India in 1883, the same year as the eruption of Krakatoa. Her father was a banker. She and her sister Kitty lived in India for their first ten years. They were very much under the influence of their Ayah, whom they loved dearly, and Marjorie learned to love India and the Indians, and enjoyed reminiscing about her Indian days. She had a large vocabulary of Hindi words which she often used. When she was ten, her father died, and she and Kitty came back to England with their mother, who is referred to as "Granny" in the letters.

Marjorie certainly didn't have an easy life, losing her father so young, living through the first world war . In 1915, she married George Tolson. Richard's father George, came from a military family, and was a Regular Army Officer. He went to Sandhurst in the first decade of the twentieth century and afterwards joined the Oxfordshire and Buckinghamshire Light Infantry. In World War I he fought in France and was severely wounded on the Somme.

The three sons were born soon after the war. Richard was the oldest. He was born on April 16th 1919. John and David were born within the next three years.

In 1923, George was appointed to the Madras Guards, and the family moved to India. With them went a very important person, "Lalla". She was not quite a nanny, not quite a maid, but she was a most loyal and devoted support to the family. For three years they lived in India, in Madras, Coonoor, and Ootacamund. Richard always described these years as idyllic, with pony rides, beaches, and delicious smells. But the time came for the boys to receive an English education, and Marjorie returned to England. It was four years before she saw her husband again. She had the task of finding a home and a school, and establishing the family in England.

They arrived at a bitterly cold Lee-on-Solent just before Christmas 1926 where they spent the first few weeks. They settled in Oxford very near the Dragon School, where Marjorie had informed the headmaster, "Hum", that he would soon be receiving her three boys. Marjorie was a resourceful woman. She was petite, pretty, wise, and tolerant and forgiving of human frailty. She was also determined to do the very best for her sons. She had the courage which belonged to her generation and bore the loss of her son John and also her husband during World War II bravely and with stoicism.

The Dragon was just the right school for Richard, for it allowed him to do the sorts of things he liked, like playing chess and singing Gilbert and Sullivan. From the Dragon, he went to Brighton College where again he was able to follow his interests. He spent much time in the library, sang in the choir, and continuing the Gilbert and Sullivan tradition, sang as leader of the chorus in the school productions. He also enjoyed his classical studies.

Richard had wanted to go into the Navy, but his parents thought this was a decision which had to be made too young – boys went to Dartmouth at fourteen – so he then decided to become a soldier. He took the examinations for The Royal Military College, Sandhurst, and passed high in the list of entrants. His first term began on Friday August 27th 1937. From that time on, he wrote regularly to his mother. All the letters begin "Dear Mummy" and end "with love from Richard" and I have omitted these words from the copies. Just a few are addressed to his father. I have also omitted some personal and family references, but I have retained original spelling and punctuation.

In 1937 war was not very far from people's minds. It was less than twenty years since end of WWI, and from July 1936 a fierce Spanish Civil War captured the imagination of a generation. Some were on the Nationalist side, which supported the Monarchy, the Church and the Army, and was led by General Francisco Franco. But the Nationalist party was not the elected Government. The Second Republic, a coalition of left and centre, had been declared in 1931. The Republicans had initiated a number of reforms, for example large estates had been broken up and land shared among the poor.

The terms are confusing, because the Nationalists, led by General Franco, were right wing but were the rebels. They were supported by the Fascist powers – Germany and Italy. Spain became a training ground for the second World War, introducing Stuka dive-bombers and storming blitzkrieg techniques with tanks. The Republicans were supported by Russia, and included many Communists. Many people from England, nearly all on the Republican side, went to fight in the war which was bloody and brutal with a high death toll, and it was the talk and concern of young men at the time. On the other hand there were many in England who thought Hitler was a safeguard against the growing Communist threat.

The first poem I have included is "Holy Holy Holy". Richard refers to "The Jesuit pimp triumphant" who "set his chain on a proud, hating and unhappy land." This is his verdict on Franco.

# HOLY, HOLY, HOLY.

It seems but yesterday
When our politicians said
'No intervention: Respect the insurgent blockade:
God, no doubt, will give them their daily bread.'
So the long agony
Of martyred Spain began and we
Piously reproved the Fascist arms:
   Our generals well wrapped up in British Warms
said 'Franco, Sir, is a gentleman, a Christian:
Christ would no doubt approve
A great intention
To restore His Holy Church –
We'll leave the bloody redshirts in the lurch.'

Sheer heroism is of no avail
Bombers and bombs, machine guns, all, reveal
That might is right and weakness only vile
   Armament manufacturers make a pile –
And the huge misery of Spain increased.
Ravaged and sterile lay the countryside
And men of every land and race and creed
Joined the lost legion of the great betrayed

So came the cruel inevitable and
The Jesuit pimp triumphant set his chains
On a proud, hating, and unhappy land.

The attitude of our Generals to the Spanish Civil War is hinted at in this poem, but I cannot be sure. I have a faint memory that Richard said he was on the wrong side when he was interviewed for Sandhurst. He wrote many letters which give a flavour of life at Sandhurst at that time. When talking about it later, he described his days as very busy, constantly having to change into different outfits. He had to work very hard at the physical training because it attracted a lot of marks. He enjoyed the academic work, but exams seem to have been almost continuous.

# 1

## Sandhurst

Royal Military College
Camberley
Surrey
February 6th 1938

Dear Mummy

I have procured some Quink, tried the pen, and formally adopted it; this is the first time I am writing with it.

We have had a very hectic week, as the first week of term always is. The subjects we are doing are quite different from last term, and we have not so many. Of course we still do Tactics, "Organisation, Administration, and Law", which we do with my Platoon officer Captain Grimston of the Queens: I don't think he's much good at teaching the stuff; also Map reading, which we do with a newly joined instructor, one Captain Barlow of the S.L.I. whom I rather like.

The Company Commander takes us for British Military History, only he will not take us for some time owing to his having contacted the rather ridiculous disease of Chicken Pox: instead we are being taken by Saunders-Jacobs until he recovers.

Car Maintenance will be quite interesting I think, though now they say we will not drive lorries until next term. We do a subject called "Imperial & International Affairs" which is very interesting, and finally my Optional Subject "Political & Economic History" from 1870 to the present day. Originally this was two separate subjects but last term the Board of Inspectors said that Political & Economic Histories should go together, so I've let myself in for more than I bargained for.

We do two periods of Equitation a week, and I am thoroughly enjoying it; later on we ride on Barrossa. [1.] There is such a lot in the afternoons now, that I never know what to do, or how to fit in everything I'm meant to do. Of course I'm meant to go down to the Palace [2.] regularly to get all my P.T. tests, and then every afternoon they expect us to be on the range practising for the inters tests; we are also in the middle of the Platoon rugger, and I am in the team for that; we have won one round of that. And of course we must turn up regularly to practice for the inter company sports; so you can imagine that I eat my lunch in ten minutes and am down on the range at 1.20 pm and thence I make the round, hoping to be finished by tea time. However it is quite good fun. Could you send me my Fishers "History of Europe" in my big book case; it will help me a lot this term.

Yesterday afternoon I was up to my neck in kit cleaning ready for the inspection on Monday. I haven't finished yet. In the evening we had Glenorchy in to play the bag pipes, which he did very well. He has only learned for a year.

On Wednesday evening I went to see the "Prisoner of Zenda" it was very good indeed.

Well, no more news.
With love from Richard

May 15th 1938

Yesterday I played cricket for the Company against Blackdown Garrison Club, and beat them by an innings and about fifty runs – a very enjoyable match, although only four members of our team had an innings, and since I was in eighth I was not one. Immediately the match finished I had to rush and change, and since it was a day of showers, I 'bus'ed with a fellow in our company called Napier, a very nice chap, into Aldershot where we saw the 'Return of the Scarlet Pimpernel', very good, 'tho not up to the standard of its predecessor. Then we found that the bus conductor had told us what time the buses back ran, but had omitted to tell us at what time they stopped running; so we embussed to Farnborough, at 5 past ten, and at 10.30 we set out to walk to the RMC in order to be in time to sign in at 11.15. It seemed a long way in the dark, and when about ¾ of a mile from home we were lucky enough to get a lift from my platoon serjeant, whom, with extraordinary luck we had chosen to stop and ask for a lift. We just got in at 11.10: a most eventful evening.

... next term we are definitely going to have to work on Saturday mornings, and there will be no week ends! I don't honestly know what this place is coming to; it is changing, very definitely for the worse. I always find that whenever I go near a place, old traditions and customs are being swept away, and totally undesirable reforms instituted.

May 26 1938

We had a Map Reading treasure hunt on Monday; all over the country, working out bearings, resection, inter-visibility problems etc. We started at 2 minute intervals; I started 2$^{nd}$, caught up no: 1, and led all the way, arriving at the end 21 minutes before everyone else. On a time basis however I was beaten by one fellow an 'A' cadet; and so only got 2$^{nd}$ prize.

I got 82% in our first Military Law paper which I believe was equal top. It is quite an interesting subject.


May 29$^{th}$ 1938

Dear Daddy,

Thank you very much for your letter and cheque for £4.11.0 enclosed. I will go and settle with Farrells tomorrow afternoon.

General Sir Ian Hamilton took the parade this morning and delivered a stirring address, remarking that we marched past far better than our Grandfathers did, and they thought they were alright! The Commandant and Uncle Bernard were with him.

A fellow in our ride had a nasty accident out on Barossa, when we were jumping the other day. He broke his arm.


"Uncle Bernard", often referred to as "Uncle B". was General Sir Bernard Paget, and Richard's Godfather. In 1941 he became Commander in Chief, Home Forces, and in 1944 was appointed general officer Commander in Chief Middle East. He was a good friend and adviser to Richard.

The following letter concerns the Dragon School. Old Dragons (O.D.s )are often referred to. A peculiarity of the Dragon, an un-stuffy school, was that the masters were known by their nick-names, whether flattering or not. "Gunga Din", a reference to Kipling, was one of the Dragon houses.

June 6th 1938

Yes, Mathias was a contemporary of mine, and since he hasn't been back since he left we decided to go over. We didn't get there in time for lunch, but we saw everybody, and I had a long chat with Tubby, Fuzz, and Francis Wylie; Then Mathias went off to see a friend, and I had tea with Jock, who plied me with questions about the RMC, and John and David.

After tea I met Hum, Mrs Hum, and Audrey, who said she was very sorry to have missed David at the O.D. Dinner. Hum was very cut up about getting no scholarships at Winchester and Eton. Mr Hum asked to be remembered to you.

I was asked to dinner by Tubby, with the staff in Gunga, but he had been asked beforehand to go and have something with Ian Burrows, you remember him at Brighton, in his rooms at Hertford. I enjoyed my visit very much, and saw everyone I possibly could, Bruno, Tortoise, Wilkinson, and Box. We caught a good train back getting in at 10.30 pm.

June 19th 1938

I hope you got back safely on Saturday. I should really have written before today, but what with it being the last week before the exams; and the last week of P.T, I haven't had much time.

Tomorrow we start off with the car maintenance exam, in which I hope to do fairly well; on Tuesday we have map reading, and Political History; on Wednesday Organisation and Administration, on Thursday Military History and Imperial & International Affairs, and on Friday the Drill Competition and Tactics.

The average group for the terms work this term is 28, and I have got group 22 which is 6 above average. The highest group is 17, but only two fellows have got that. I have got 84% in my P.T. and with a little luck I might bring it up to 90% in the last week.

I bathed twice in the bathing lake last week, and also sunbathed. The lake is very popular in this weather, and hundreds of people spend their whole afternoon down there.

I got a group 1 in another History essay we did last week, which was top marks.

There is really not much news: Everyone is getting terrified at the thought of exams, for no one seems to have done much work. The concert on Tuesday went off very well, as did the refreshments supplied after it.

Our Equitation test is in the last week; I hear that it is not at all difficult.

Undated

The weather has taken a change for the worse: Howling gales and rain.

Yes, if there ever is a war it is far better to join up as an officer and have a course of training here.

The next letter mentions Hugh Easton. He was at school with Richard at Brighton, and went with him to Sandhurst. Hugh's sister Joan later married Richard's brother David.

September 19th 1938

Thank you very much for your letter; sorry mine is a day overdue, but the strain of work is terrific. I have just finished one essay, have got two more to do for next week, as well as a lecture which I may be called upon to give in Military History next week; the subject is an extensive one, "Influence of Administration on the Palestine campaign up to October 31$^{st}$ 1917".

In view of an apparently imminent possibility I have taken up lessons in the German language, which I hope may be of use to me: My mentor, Napier, says I show great promise and a definite flair for languages, a fact which has so far lain unrecognised by my many instructors in French, Latin, and Greek.

A most unpleasant incident happened during an equitation period last week: Our instructor, an amiable man was put under arrest by the Cavalry R.S.M, who is universally unpopular, for taking us hacking.

Everyone in the battalion loathes the Equitation R.S.M so when he came to the Company to collect evidence we gave him a hot reception, booed and hissed him, and made him generally uncomfortable. Of course we like an occasional quiet ride, so those who were interrogated were quite willing to perjure their souls, and so the fellow couldn't prove his charge and our instructor got off. It made the European crisis quite unimportant when it was on.

I went out to tea with Easton and family yesterday; they brought his sister down to see a parade. I sat next to the Company Commander last band night; he was alright to talk to, and I hope I have created a more favourable impression, though why he is not fond of me I cannot think! Rugger practice has at last started, tho' I can't think why; the ground is hard as iron.

Unfortunately I was not elected President of the Debating Society: Last terms secretary was; I think he will be very good.

Hope John [Richard's brother] will write and tell me how he likes the business, and what Hilary's dance was like.


The next letter was written at the time of the Munich crisis. Germany was gradually encroaching on more and more neighbouring territory. The Rhineland and Austria had already been absorbed as "lebensraum" by Hitler, who claimed that he needed more space for the German people. The Sudetanland had a largely German population, and was another excuse for the invasion of Czeckoslovakia in 1938. In August that year it seemed that we were on the brink of war. The Prime Minister, Neville Chamberlain, went to Germany and came to an agreement with Hitler: this was to be positively his last encroachment on other territory. Chamberlain returned, waving a piece of paper and saying "peace with honour". People were divided over this. No-one wanted war so soon after the horrors of WWI. We were poorly prepared, and Chamberlain speeded up rearmament. But many felt we had behaved disgracefully to Czeckoslovakia.

October 2ⁿᵈ 1938

Thank you for all your letters last week which I had to answer in such an unsatisfactory manner. The course of events seems now to be definitely set towards a peaceful issue, at any rate we are returning to our normal routine tomorrow morning, and everyone is disappointed that it is so; it has been a really wonderful week here, 'tho it may sound rather selfish and callous to say so.

Last Monday morning everything was going on as usual, and I had no inkling that anything really serious was happening, when suddenly after lunch everyone was confined to the buildings, and we were told that normal routine had been abandoned until further notice and trench digging was to begin in the evening. We dug fast and furiously, my hands were a mass of blisters, and when we finished at 7.15 pm we returned to the Company, and found that all the windows had shutters up, that no lights were to be shown in the bathrooms, and various other uncomfortable precautions. Tuesday morning we all dug again up to lunch, and we began again after lunch: our Platoon had been chosen as the fire fighting platoon, and much to my pleasure I was given a section.

Our duty during a raid was to put out any fires that broke out; a responsible job, and we were duly initiated into the intricacies of the college fire fighting machine. After mess we had a mock alarm; everyone had to get to their places in full equipment; for most of the Company this was merely in basement under the Company, but we had to trudge in Greatcoats, Gas masks, and carrying cushions to the other end of the building in order to be near the fire station. 3 sections were bundled into a tiny gas proof room and we were informed that we might have to stay there 36 hrs in the event of a raid; we were nearly boiled alive in the hour we were down there.

Tuesday night was also band night, and we only had a dim religious light to eat by and I think nearly everyone thought that it would be our last band night, so everyone promptly got into debt by signing drinks they could'nt afford, and we had a grand singsong towards the end, after the King.

Wednesday morning while others dug, our Platoon practised putting out fires; it is no joke having to run half a mile in a gas mask carrying heavy hose pipe and sundry picks and shovels, especially when you are in command of 6 other fellows whom you have to direct.

In the afternoon and evening we dug again, half holiday was cancelled, this time trenches dug down by the Married Quarters. On Friday and yesterday we were constructing barricades against shell bursts round the entrance to the gymnasium, which is the Casualty Clearing Station for Camberley. By Friday as you know things got better and we were given a half holiday and D. O. leave. I should say the whole R.M.C. went to Aldershot and coming back in the last 'bus we were all G.C.s except for three civilians who looked terrified; we had rousing choruses all the way back, and thoroughly enjoyed ourselves.

And now we are faced with a terrific anticlimax;

everyone was working so well together, and all the usual pettiness went out of this place; I expect you know what I mean. The officers all helped digging the trenches, and in the Platoon everything went with a swing. It seems a pity that as soon as we are confronted with peace the Seniors suddenly remember what dignified and superior people they are, etc, etc.

We were told by the adjutant that if war were declared the senior division would move out immediately, so perhaps it is as wise to have the boxes done up in case anything happens.

I hope Daddy is allowed to resume normal work again; I suppose he will now.

I feel very sorry for the Czechs: Although I think Chamberlain has done magnificently, it appears to be only a temporary measure; Hitler wants Prague.

Yesterday I helped decorate the chapel for the Harvest Thanksgiving Service which we had this morning. We had to display all the goods provided by 5 Company, which go to various hospitals.

Very pleasant to get the extra hour this morning; I have slept very soundly all this week, in spite of the various night alarms.


October 16th 1938
Dear Daddy


Thank you very much for your letter. John Jones is listed as one of the Tailors to the 35th, so I expect it will be alright; they are about the only tailors from whom I have not had about five begging letters, all of whom, it would appear, have only my interests at heart, and all holiday the opinion that I have little hope of salvation if I patronise any rival firm.

I believe that it is usual for us to get about a months leave after the date on which we are gazetted, which is Jan 26th. Of course it does not always apply, some fellows last term had to join within a fortnight, but it is usual to get a month; something to do with pay I suppose.

Well having heard all my marks I have reached an average of 64.6, and while it is not as good as last half term, yet in proportion with the marks of other fellows it is better; the papers really were quite hard. Funnily enough I obtained 162 / 200 in my Car Maintenance and 139 / 200 in Political History, both were quite good marks, and I think I will be moved up to the 2nd or 3rd set in Car Maintenance.

I have played a little tennis, and had some cricket nets, 'tho there have been no league games so far.

Thank you for the Draconian which was very interesting: I liked Bruno's verse. Did David enjoy the OD dinner; I suppose he stayed the night at the school, and not with Henry Alden.

They have at last begun voluntary riding so in future I hope to get a little more of it in the afternoon.


Dates were very important to both Richard and his mother. Birthdays were never forgotten, and several historic dates are remembered – Trafalgar Day, Waterloo, and Quebec Day – a Regimental honour – among them.

November 3rd 1938

Many happy returns for your birthday tomorrow; I do hope you will like the gloves from John and myself, and that they match the new fur coat. I had a quick journey up to Town, and arrived at Fentons flat where I had much sustenance, liquid and solid. We had a good journey down to Camberley, 'tho every one was terribly depressed at coming back here. So far we have only had one exam paper back, the Military History paper, and I scored 71%, bringing me within the first half dozen; if I get the same in the other papers I ought to be quite alright. There seems to be not much news at present, as we have not done much since we came back.

I will write again on Sunday; also to John. Did you enjoy 'Snow White' on Wednesday? I hope so.


November 6th 1938

I hope you had a very happy birthday and that my letter got home by the first post, as I posted it rather late.

We have had two more results since I last wrote. Indoor and Outdoor Tactics; in the written I got 78%, and in the outdoor 69%, which was fairly good; I was afraid I might have messed up the outdoor, as some fellows did. Captain King was very pleased with the results as we had the highest company average.

I fenced in the assault at arms for the company last week. The captain of the team was asked to send in a team of three for foil, and he put us down in any order with my name at the top; imagine my horror when I found that because of this I was fighting first string, while Johnson who is a fencing blue fought only second. I found myself up against some good fencers, and out of the 3 fights I won 1, and lost two. A pity because I might have won more if I had fought 2$^{nd}$ string, my proper place.

I am going out to dinner tonight with Captain Clapham, a gunner, whom I meet a lot at the musical society; very nice of him to ask me; I think we are going to sing after dinner.

November 14$^{th}$ 1938

At last we have the results of all our exams; Optional Subject 63%, Military Law 81%, Organisation & Administration 70%, Book keeping 72%, Imperial & International Affairs 68%, Car Maintenance 65%, Theoretical Tactics 78%, Outdoor Tactics 69%; altogether it makes an average Mark of about 69% with Military History 71%. Ten of our seniors have been put on the Black list.

I went out to tea yesterday with Shoosmith who lives at Yateley, and I met a Colonel Muirhead of the Northamptons who was an instructor at Sandhurst about the same time as Daddy; he remembers Daddy very well and asked to be remembered to him: He lives at Yateley.

I commanded a section in platoon training last week, and at any rate did not make any mistakes. All beagling has been stopped here owing to foot and mouth disease; I expect it is rife in David's part of the world also.

No more news, I think the huns ought to be massacred.

November 20ᵗʰ 1938

We had our big Military History debate on Easterners v Westerners, on Friday, and I have discovered that I am a quite convincing speaker; I held the 'house' for about ten minutes, and made, I think, some good points, heaping ridicule on the Easterners who had made some thumping mistakes in their set speeches; anyway everyone shrieked with laughter at them, and a fellow told me that the Company Commander had laughed all through dinner, at band night in the new buildings; and everyone said it was the best speech of the evening: Yesterday our terms grouping for Military History came out and I find I have a group 2, which is the highest given; no one getting a group 1; so I'm glad I spoke.

Now the weather has changed again and it is very cold and raining hard; a horrid day. This evening I am going to the RMC flick to see "The Informer" which I believe is good.

I have been asked to take part in a variety show, which is being given on the night before the dance in the RMC theatre; it is a slapdash thing and does'nt take up much time rehearsing, so I felt that I could accept.

November 28ᵗʰ 1938

Thank you for your letter. There seems to be very little news this week; I think the dreadful propinquity of the passing out exams accounts for it; in fact everyone seems to be working hard – yesterday an OB friend of Eastons came down in his car and we went out to lunch, and showed him over the stables etc. Tonight Sir Thomas Inskip[3.] comes down for the debate which is on 'That the army should take more interest in politics'. I am speaking against it, not that I necessarily believe my point of view. On Thursday we are giving the usual Choral Society concert, including a Negro Spiritual, one of Stanfords 'Songs of the Sea', and the Road to the Isles.

On Sunday we were inspected by General Stevens of the Rifle Brigade, Bert, my servant, was full of him, saying how he used to lead his regiment over the top at Ypres.

Equitation is very dull nowadays as we are doing all the sort of school drill for the passing out exam in equitation.

Up to the teeth in work! I never realised we had such a lot to get through.

December 6th 1938

I hope you got my PC yesterday. I'm very sorry to be so late with the letter but we are absolutely in the thick of it. Yesterday we had two exams, 'Section leading', written, and Equitation, in two parts, practical, and oral. I had a horse of my own choosing for the riding, and 'tho rather frisky we got on alright; the test was fairly easy, only two jumps. I think I did quite well, but do not know my marks: In the oral , which was held in the evening, I got exactly 90%, getting all the answers right except one. The section leading paper was alright except that we were very rushed for time. Now we have no more exams until next Monday when we have eight, lasting from Monday to Thursday evening.

I had quite a surprise the other day when I was told that I might quite likely go to Egypt in February; all regulations about spending a year in England have been cancelled, so I may quite likely find myself out there; it will be very nice as I always wanted to join the 35th on first appointment.

The concert went off very well on Thursday; we were beaten up in the Rugger and Soccer against the Shop[4] on Saturday, but won the Equitation and the Squash. The Rugger was very disappointing to watch. An OB came down with a lot of other cadets from H.M.S Erebus to watch rugger etc, and we had tea with him afterwards. He said the RMC was luxury compared with the Erebus – they have to get up at 6.15. He is coming to the end of term dance.

Tomorrow we have a kit inspection in preparation for the Drill competition on Friday; I am surrounded by kit cleaning apparatus, and a beautiful bayonet scabbard which I have just cleaned, and in which you can see the reflection of your eyebrows.

General Sir Reginald May is taking the Salute at the Inspection parade: He was Commandant before Fisher.

December 11th 1938

I am very thankful that everything is at last arranged; for the last few weeks there has hardly been a room going, and yesterday I actually had a letter from the Camberley Court Hotel, saying that owing to cancellations they had 3 rooms empty: But I refused as the boys rooms are in a house almost on the corner of Edward Avenue, which is the first road on the right after the Harcourt House Hotel.

The girls dresses can be sent to H.H.H, Frimley Road, as soon as they like. I have ordered dinner for eight at 8 o'clock at the Harcourt.

Friday is a free afternoon for me so shall I see you first, or shall I change and meet the party at the Hotel and then guide the boys on to their lodgings; I think perhaps that would be best, although the house is only 100 feet away – but let me know times etc.

The dance is at 9.30; all tickets were sold out within the first day of their being on sale so I was lucky to have got mine immediately.

I have ordered and fitted all the necessary uniform at Jones and Stallwood. We have been told to get absolute minimum as there is a new dress order coming out.

The idea of going abroad does'nt affect me only, nor is it especially likely to affect me, only we have been told that any of us are likely to be posted straight abroad, as the year in England rule has been suspended. Napier, I know for certain, is going to Poona.

Well, this is the last day before the exams, and I must work; Tomorrow we start with Imperial & International Affairs, and Military Law, and I am attending a revision class for the former subject tonight. I have got a bad cold and nearly lost my voice, but getting better now.

# 2

## First Postings – Devonport and Belfast

Richard passed out of Sandhurst in December 1938, and joined his Regiment, The Royal Sussex, in February 1939. His first posting was to Devonport. Later they moved to Belfast.

The Royal Sussex Regiment
North Raglan Barracks,
Devonport.
Telephone 712

February 24th 1939

Just a line to let you know I arrived safely and was met at the station by an army car. It is topping here and I am thoroughly enjoying it. I am in temporary command of 'C' Company as Major Lane is on leave and the other officers are on courses. I have one S.R.Officer from whom I took over today.

Last night was band night and a pretty rollicking one too. Tonight I and three other officers are going to some sort of Naval 'Do', which I hope will be interesting – and something more.

I've just been interrupted in writing this as a fellow arrived to call on the Mess and I, being the only person in here at the time, have had to do the honours – still I hope you get this in time.

## SONNET: FREEDOM'S SONG

Men say that Homer's nodding: Who are we
To take upon ourselves an argument
To prove a falsehood. Soon they will repent
Their insolence, for we will make them see
The might accrued from doing A.R.P.
We are prepared: Poseidon was our shield
But we have now a mightier power to wield,
That unremitting Aegis, liberty.
Historic island! To yourself you take
A heavy burden, heavier than before.
Then guard it, keep it for thy conscience sake.
And, if a country alien to your love
Should seek your fall, and freedom's – Mars awake!
And fight triumphant by our native shore.

Saturday, Feb. 11th 1939

March 6th 1939

This last week has been a pretty hectic one: to begin
off with I was vice president in the Mess, which
does not entail any arduous duties; only proposing
the King, etc. On Monday I was detailed to the
Quarter Masters branch to be shown round the
Mob stores, and how various affairs are transacted.
The QM is really very nice, and began life as a
drummer boy in this Battalion. On Tuesday five of
us went out with the C.O. and did a small Tactical
scheme, in order, I think to find out exactly how
much I know – or don't know.

Wednesday I was Subaltern of the day which includes being present at all the men's meals, inspection of barracks, issue of rations etc, turning out the quad, inspecting the men on extra instructional drill; in the Regiment you are always Subalterns of day for two consecutive days, which is pretty dreadful. On Wednesday and Friday we went on a scheme with Major Lane my Company Commander, and we went out to Roborough Common, the beginnings of Dartmoor in the Baby Austins. I drove one and they are very useful little cars. I have taken up bayonet fencing in order to go in for the individual competition; and had my first lesson on Friday. It is a rather clumsy sport, and doesn't give you the same satisfaction as when handling a foil – however I persevere, to the extent of fencing every morning of the week at 7.15 am.

Now that Major Lane is back I have been detailed to command no 14 Platoon – and a more dunderheaded bunch of ignorant idle yokels it would be hard to find. Actually they are very good fellows, and most of them try hard – but nearly all are just come from the depot and are not quite up to standard. Some of the kit is a disgrace, but I am doing my best to brace things up. The trouble is that the Platoon has been without an officer for some time.

My batman, Cooper, is one of the best servants in the place. He learns everything I teach him, always has the right clothes put out, lights the fire well. He lives in Hove, so knows Brighton very well. He is taking his 2nd class Certificate of Education, and I suppose he will want to get promoted, and give up his present job.

I have called on the immediately pressing people, but have not yet called on the Booths, as the only afternoon we get off is Saturday, with an occasional Wednesday.

Yesterday I went riding with Cardwell at Chagford. A lovely spot thirty miles north of Plymouth on the far side of Dartmoor. We rode on the moors, had the biggest tea I've ever (?) had, and coming back ran into a Dartmoor fog. We stopped at a 15th century moorland Pub which was miles from anywhere, and was lit with oil lamps. Luckily the fog was only in places so we just got back in time.

March 12th 1939

I was on Church parade this morning for the first time and everything went off quite well. I don't think much of the padre here, he talked the most terrific bilge in his sermon; however most people had ten minutes sleep so it was alright.

I am orderly officer tomorrow and Tuesday, the bayonet fighting is now changed to Wednesday, and there is an 'all ranks' dance on Thursday at which we put in an appearance.

I am wondering whether it is worth while trying to get over and see the Yeo's sometime, although time and the weather make it rather impossible. The other night I went to see a variety show in Plymouth, with four other chaps, and it included Alice Delysia[1], who I regret to say was really pathetic. She tried to sing a lot of her old songs, but she is very large now, and they don't suit her.

I am temporarily Battalion Sports Officer as Captain Le Mesurier has gone on leave, and I suppose he thought I was the most likely to do it, 'tho there is very little to be done.

March 12<sup>th</sup> 1939

Dear Daddy

Thank you for your letter of some time ago. I am very glad to hear that you have been elected President of the 'Old Contemptibles' [2] at Aylesbury.

I am surprised that they have been so quick in crediting me with my ration allowance for my months leave. I went and saw the orderly room soon after I arrived and they said I might get it in about a months time.

The messing here is 3/6 per diem, and is not at all bad. There is a fair amount of drinking, and the charges for drink are pretty steep. Next week, or rather the week after next we are having a lot of bigwigs to dine, the Admiral Dunbar-Nasmith, and Major General Green.

Next Thursday nine of us are going on a visit of instruction to the 8<sup>th</sup> Battalion of the Royal Tank Corps at Perham Down. We are leaving Plymouth at the incredible hour of 5 am; taking breakfast, and having supper somewhere on the way back.

March 19<sup>th</sup> 1939

Great news – I believe I can get leave from Friday March 31<sup>st</sup> until Monday evening. I am putting in my application tomorrow, but I am practically certain it will be granted – so I hope you have got a spare ticket for David's show.

If I come up I shall come by car, as another fellow is coming up then and is only too glad to share the petrol – and I will be able to relieve him at the wheel occasionally. Of course it will be a long journey but it will save a lot on train fares.

On Thursday we all went on an instructional visit to the 8th Battalion R.T.C at Perham Down which is just beyond Tidworth – a good 150 miles there. The more senior officers went in the COs car and we were fated to get in a bus with the serjeants – I knew I would feel very ill, so Hugh Taylor, a very nice fellow and one of our senior subalterns offered to take three of us in his car. We left here at 5.30 am and stopped for breakfast at the Digby Hotel Sherborne.

We got to Perham Down at 10.15 and learned all about tanks until 1.15 – I went in an 'I' tank, and frankly I feel very very sorry for the poor wretches who are fated to ride in them in war time. On the other hand I realise now that these modern tanks are very difficult indeed to see even when the only background is a gorse common. On the other hand, one was very easily ditched in a shallow trench, and nothing would get it out. My own ride I quite enjoyed, swivelling about in a turret, looking out through a periscope, although you cannot see a great deal.

After our labour we had lunch in the mess and…. I met a fellow who was in 5 Company, and a term senior to me. He was on the Young Officers course at Netheravon and said he thought I would be on it soon. I also met a fellow of my own term who was on the course because both Battalions of his regiment were abroad.

After lunch, at about 3.15 we started home, and stopped for tea at Sherborne at the same place. Hugh Taylor was at school there and wanted to see various people, so I thought I would go and look up Jerry Henderson. I went to his house and found him out, so a very nice chap sent someone to find him, and told me all about the various Dragons at Sherborne. Then Jerry came in and was quite astounded to see me. He asks to be remembered you Daddy, and Lalla, and remembered her coconut ice from the Old Bardwell Rd days. Then Taylor came in and wanted to see Jerry's housemaster, so I was pushed along too and introduced as an O.D. We had a glass of sherry and found that we had many mutual acquaintances.

Eventually we got on our way, stopping for dinner at Honiton, and getting back about 11pm – an eventful day.

Yesterday evening I went to dinner with the Booths, and met a gunner who is adjutant of a Coast Defence unit. Philip thinks there will be war at any moment, and says he dreads every telephone bell. He had some Port which was 61 years old which we drank with the deference due to its age, 'tho it had lost its essential flavour.

Well, no more news – lets hope the situation clears – 'tho that devil ought to be provided for in no uncertain fashion.

March 26th 1939

Thank you very much for your letter. This has been an energetic week and the coming one is going to be even more so. Tomorrow we are going out with full war equipment for the whole day, march about ten miles, dig some weapon pits, and march back. On Tuesday we are having a parade for the G.O.C, and on Wednesday we are all going to be gassed – why, I dont know. There is a Serjeants Mess dance tomorrow evening, and a Regimental Guest night on Tuesday evening. On Thursday we are giving a sherry party, and at last on Friday afternoon some time we will set out for home. I dont expect we will get back until the evening, and I ought perhaps to be back in time for a late dinner. We have only got leave from after duty on Friday, so we ought to leave here about 2pm. I suppose it will take six hours to get up by car.

I went to the All Ranks dance on Friday, and it was quite amusing. I got there about 10 pm. It wasn't a very crowded dance as a lot of men were on leave. However I danced a little, having been introduced to various Sergeants wives, but spent most of the time with the sergeants – you know where. All the officers turned up except the three SROs which wasn't too good. This evening I am playing squash, as I have been lazy all today.

This morning we paraded with the local 'Old Contemptibles' who attended church parade. There were four VCs on parade, including the CO.

I have become assistant messing officer and now choose the daily menus with Captain Le Mesurier. The first thing I had to arrange was dinner for my own dining in.

I don't know if the crisis [3] is now spent, but I think it is pretty shameful doing absolutely nothing while our damned politicians squabble about the ethics of the case. I should scrap them all and put in old Churchill.

April 9th 1939

Well I hope you don't think that I have disappeared off the face of the earth. I meant to write earlier but first of all lost my fountain pen, now found, and the chaos of packing is inconceivable. I was only given half a days notice to get my boxes packed and thought we had until the tenth. However my servant did wonders and I now live in a very empty room.

I am writing like this as an experiment, to see if you can read this method of crossed writing as our ancestors did. We were rather late getting back to Plymouth as we were travelling behind another car which, for no reason at all went straight into another car – luckily no one was hurt. Today, I am orderly officer and everyone else has a holiday. I took a party of men to church and we had an unbelievably cheerful service, the Padre being a man without imagination. I had hoped to go to a performance of the 'Messiah' this evening, but I'm afraid it will be impossible unless I get someone to do my job for a few hours – which is unlikely.

In April the Regiment moved to Belfast, which became one of Richard's favourite cities. War seemed imminent, and training was vigorous. In March, Hitler occupied the rest of Czeckoslovakia. Quite why Richard felt moved to write about the death of Princess Tatiana, one of the daughters of Tzar Nicholas, on St George's day I am not sure. At that time, Russia still had a pact with Hitler, and the vengeance he refers to is perhaps the vengeance against both our enemies.

April 16th 1939
[Belfast]

Dear Aunt Kitty,

Thank you very much for your present for my birthday; I had an enormous mail yesterday, which was very cheering in this barbarous but charming country. We had a very good journey up by train from Devonport and then by sea from Heysham, the whole journey taking abut eighteen hours.

Have you seen anything about us in the papers? Of course the Belfast papers have been writing about us for days, and have made up some wonderful statements about us.

April 16ᵗʰ 1939
[Belfast]

Dear Grannie

Thank you ever so much for your birthday present, which will adorn one of the walls of my room.

I have just come in from a long exploration of the country side which is very beautiful, 'tho owing to the amount of rain it is exceedingly boggy too.

Please remember me to the Parrot.

St George's Day 1939

It has come; it is arrived! Even now I am listening to Sandy MᶜPherson playing Handel's Largo – and playing it quite well: all of which is to say that not only has it arrived safely, but has been set up by one of my friends, and is going marvellously; it is a great solace, especially as I am orderly officer today. Thank you all again very much, it is a grand present. Woe is me, that I cannot take it to camp.

My room is now looking quite civilised; I have bought some rather nice stuff which the tailor is making into curtains, which matches very well the colour of the wall paper which is just a shade darker than that in my room at home. My servant is busy painting my windows and sills a delicate cream colour, instead of the white (a very dirty white) which they are now. The room is slightly smaller than at Devonport, and has not quite so much clothes space, but on the whole it is much nicer.

Belfast has three good theatres and at the Opera House on Wednesday I saw 'Spring Meeting' with Lena Dan. It was one of the best comedies I have seen, and we all thoroughly enjoyed it. Next week they have the 'Maid of the Mountains' which of course I will be unable to see.

Since we have been here I have got to know my 'almost contemporaries' much better, and they are all jolly good chaps: Holmwood, one of the last joined before me, dropped in late one night, and I found out that I knew his best friend, who was at Brighton with me, and is now in the navy: moreover his own father was at Brighton, and knew H.B. quite well. And Harris, of the same term as Holmwood, is above six foot four: he is in my company, very nice, 'tho rather vacuous.

I am marching the company down to the station tomorrow as Harris will be arranging things at the station, and Lane is going by car. I have been appointed Sports Officer for the camp, and have got together a formidable array of sports impedimenta, tug of war ropes, hockey sticks, cricket bats, javelins, and disci: So we are going to live a strenuous life. Even in barracks we all have to turn up for PT at 6.55 every day except Sunday, but so far the weather has been lovely, and I haven't minded it; today, alas, the rains have come – what price camp!

# EPITAPH ON THE
# PRINCESS TATIANA OF RUSSIA

Fair lovely girl, sweet April's sweeter bride
Peerless in faith, rejoiced in Russia's pride.
Who never wronged, who never cruel spoke
Whom nature, in her bounty, made awake
To see the earth, the trees, the radiant sky,
The waters clear, the beasts, the birds to fly.
And Nature's hard, but man is cruel far,
And grosser man is only made to mar
The tenderness, that higher worth will strive,
In knowledge of itself, to make alive.


Ah cruel fate; earth's fearless princess laid
Cold to the ground. The price is dearly paid.
But blood calls blood, and vengeance follows sure
To stamp upon the slayer of the pure.
Her name will live, the honoured martyr's cause
Will win more victories than many wars.

1939 St George's Day


(Note added 24 – 8 – '39 —— "vengeance is about to
be paid")

Magilligan Camp
Nt Bellarina
Co Derry
N Ireland

Monday May 1st

Thank you very much for your letter which arrived rather late here. The post man only comes when he feels like it, which isn't often.

We have had an extremely hectic week, and quite literally we were never off duty until Saturday after lunch. We left Belfast by train on Monday morning, arriving here for lunch, and from 3 o'clock until 6.15 I was out on the range superintending final preparations. The air is wonderful, the scenery delightful, the weather glorious, but the night cold is intense – so cold is it that the ice has had to be broken off our washing water in the morning.

I consider we lead a Spartan existence; cold water to wash in, up at six, lunch, if you're lucky at 2 pm, and finally off the ranges at 6 oclock, followed by Rifle inspections, Bren gun inspections etc etc. By the time I have consumed an enormous dinner and played a few hands of Whist, I am ready for my arctic tent.

I am now in charge of Messing (for the Companies) and this is a very full job, as it has been allowed to get in a bad state. However it is a good experience and I am enjoying it.

Yesterday I organised a cricket match v 'A' company, we won; I went in and made 5.

This is very hasty as I must catch the lorry to 'Derry.

## May 7th 1939 – Camp near Derry

We are having a hectic time now, as an epidemic of German Measles broke out on Tuesday: At first it was thought to be Scarlet Fever, and was diagnosed as such, then on Friday the doctor, a typical Irishman discovered that it was, in reality, the Ayrian form of measles. If any more cases result we will probably stay here over our time, which will suit me, as this is an entirely admirable place, it has Devon beat to a frazzle.

I have organised and captained a 'C' company team, cricket – and so far we have played three matches, won one, tied one, and drawn one. The men enjoy playing cricket very much and we have some quite good players. I have received a challenge from Bellarina C.C. but have declined for medical reasons – a pity. Today I journeyed into Derry, and had an interesting day. I looked up Webb at Ebrington Barracks but he has gone to camp near Limarady. The ban confining us to Camp was lifted last night, and Peter Rubie drove four of us at about 85 mph to Limarady to toast the occasion. I had a letter from Donald Low the other day: He wants to be my batman for six months; I told him he was the last person in the world I should chose to look after me.

The Messing is going very well and Major Prince expressed his approval yesterday. No sooner had he done so than the RASC failed to supply us with today and tomorrow's meat ration, owing to a railway breakdown: Luckily we had enough tucked away for today's dinner meal, and the truck went in to Derry this morning and the meat had arrived, so a delicate situation was saved. The firing is going very well, and I am a 1st class Bren gunner.

Victoria Barracks, Belfast
May 14th 1939

Well I am very sorry that our time at Magilligan is finished; it was great fun, and in the last week especially, we thoroughly enjoyed it. I am several shades browner than when we first went there, and it isn't dirt.

On Monday my platoon was the one chosen, by virtue of a good shoot, from the company, to go in for the Hopton Cup on Wednesday. We had plenty of opportunity to run through as I was allowed to have my men and the range whenever necessary. We got a score of 135 on the day, which wasn't too bad considering that two of the shooters only arrived from the depot in April, and one not long before that: The score was the best we had obtained.

On Thursday night I was out with A company on night firing and finished at 1 am and on Friday night I had to organise and command the company for our own night shoot, which included firing on fixed lines by the LMH, and a competition between three sections in night firing under realistic conditions, smoke was used to represent gas, and innumerable toy bombs and fireworks which were let off all round the sections. The first phase of the competition was firing at flashes, and the second at advancing figure 2's with Verey lights to illuminate the scene. It was very exciting and everyone thoroughly enjoyed it I think.

I have ended up the Messing with £5.18.0 credit balance and £4 worth of stock in hand so I feel I haven't done too badly as we were in debt when camp started. Yesterday we left Magilligan and I was in command of the Ammunition and Arms train which consisted of three 3 ton lorries;

it rained all the way back, and when we got in there were no fatigue parties to offload us: I was furious, especially as the Serjeant Major said he would attend personally to it. However I soon rooted everyone out and all was well.

It was very pleasant to get back to a large comfortable bed, and a fire, and a wireless, and I am now just going to enjoy a quiet afternoon – the first for some time.

I have been attached to the Intelligence Section for their fortnights training in July, and I believe it is most interesting, running about in Austins all over the countryside. The Mess is now done up and properly furnished and is very pleasant; the nicest Mess I have seen. In view of the conscripts[4] huts are being erected in every nook and cranny in barracks, and soon there will be no parade ground. We are promising ourselves a great time with the conscripts: a Battalion up to and over strength – rapture.

May 21st 1939

I am sending a snap taken when we were marching from Bellarina Station to the camp; I think it has come out very well. The chap on my left with the funny walk is our C.S.M, Cracknell, a very good man, and the chap on the right, with a foolish looking cap is Cp. Maker. The snap was taken by Harris with one of those tiny cameras, and I never thought it would come out.

Yesterday I captained a (not 'the') Battalion cricket team against the RASC. We were trying out newcomers and lost the match by fifty runs. I scored 12 not out, which is good for me, I expected to come out first ball. The garrison Cricket Ground is delightful, completely surrounded by trees, you would never think you were in the centre of Belfasts poor area. It was also a lovely cricket day, so what matters the defeat!

On Wednesday, Thursday, and Friday, I was out all day going over the training ground for company training in July: I have made up four schemes, which is very interesting, much more so than carrying them out. Kilroot is about 12 miles from Belfast, the ground is very good and the farmers very pleasant.

I saw the 'Citadel' last Monday, and thought it was very good, 'tho not quite as good as I expected. I played a great game of Chess one night which lasted until 12.30 and even then we stopped in the middle and called it a draw: Funnily enough Holmwood had been taught to play by Storr Best the Maths master at Brighton.

The band left last week for England to begin their engagement season, so we have no band to play in Mess now.

On Tuesday afternoon Harris and I went for a tour in his Singer and visited Downpatrick, where St Patrick is buried, and went right down the coast to the Mourne Mountains which are lovely: They go straight up from the sea like this. You would never believe it if you hadn't seen them, complete sugar loaves and very steep. We came back through the mountain pass, with a number of hair pin bends.

I am Company Sports Officer, and in the absence of Le Mesurier, battalion Sports officer, and also assisting with the cricket, so I foresee a full time ahead. Battalion sports are to be run on 7th and 8th of June.

# Whit Monday 1939

This Whitsun we have been having a really good holiday: Saturday, and Monday completely free. On Monday I went with Rich to the Royal Ulster Agricultural Show which was very good indeed. It included a wonderful Horse Show, jumping competition etc, with the band of the Irish Guards – which is appallingly bad – and all sorts of stands, flowers, commercial vehicles, threshers, ploughs, as well as a miniature 'Ideal Home Exhibition' in the central Hall. There was an army stand, run by the Regiment, and except for an ice cream stand, it was the most patronised of them all.

Yesterday Harris and I took a picnic lunch and went on a tour through Ulster in his car. We visited Lough Neagh, had our lunch in a field nearby, visited Armagh, the tiny city with two enormous Cathedrals, and then went on through Co. Tyrone to Co. Fermanagh to Enniskillan, the most beautiful country in Ireland, we went along the N side of the Lough which is the longest in Ireland – get out your map please – and stopped at a Hotel – the Lough Erne Hotel, about seven miles out of Enniskillan, and had a large 'high tea', and wandered down to the Lough. It was incredibly hot – a perfect day.

Very reluctantly we left at seven o'clock, then up to Omagh and then, very rashly we tried a short cut across the Sperrin Mts; we then learned what Irish roads are really like – we never went over 20 miles an hour, and in addition got completely lost – we didn't get out of those mountains until 9.30 pm, and I drove the rest of the way home. We went 220 miles, not bad going.

Every bit of Ulster seems so different, yet every part is lovelier than the other, at least that is what it seems like when you are travelling through.

This afternoon we have a Company cricket match on – glorious weather again. On Tuesday we settle down to routine; I am not going to camp with 'A' Company, so will be in Barracks until July 3rd. There is not much to do in Barracks, so I am reading up all my manuals, and J.T. and FSR, as well as making up schemes on paper, which may be put into practice later on.

I see that two divisions are passing out of the RMC this term – only a precaution I suppose. I hope John's Motorbike is going well; I never knew he had to pass another test to ride it. Did you win anything on the Derby? I won 2/11ᵈ from an 'each way' bet on Fox Cub, it would have been more only I lost another bet on Iriguero.

June 28th 1939

I have had a most satisfying week; Three cricket matches, one lost, one drawn, and one won. At last I am really getting things to move, and I had nets every spare night of the week. I have made a thorough nuisance of myself, impressing upon the Orderly Room and the PRI the National Importance of Cricket to the morale and physical well-being of the nation – and the army in particular – in this present time of disturbance, and have managed to get the cricket team off Route Marches on thursdays, if we are playing on that day, and, more important, I have got a complete new set of cricket shirts, flannels, balls, etc, from the PRI, no small feat I assure you.

The Reservists have turned up trumps, and are not only good cricketers, but damned keen, and the Colonel, and Major Prince have both been playing regularly lately. On Wednesday we were beaten by Queens University; on Thursday we drew with Campbell College. It was a damned good game, a lovely ground, and a perfect day, so what more could we ask; the result was a draw because of time; we might have beaten them but personally I did not think we would. On Saturday we beat Woodvale C.C., and my fast bowler did the hat trick – it was amazing; three men clean bowled. Our fixture list is now so full, that being Battalion Cricket Officer has become more than a spare time job, and since there are now only four subalterns in the Battalion, and plenty of routine work to do, I don't finish till about 7.30 pm, if you count nets as work.

However I am thoroughly enjoying it all, and I think I ought to get a good chit this year. Harris, my immediate senior has been suddenly sent abroad, to the 35th [5], he leaves us on Tuesday. That means that I am the next to go abroad, probably in September; I don't see why you should be worried at my going, after all the 35th was the Regiment I wanted to go into, and I am sure there's more soldiering abroad than here.

Would you like a copy of the Roussillon Gazette?[6] I have just got mine. One of my Platoon corporals wrote our Platoon notes; I was amused to see this about me, "We welcome 2/Lieut RGS Tolson and …. already we feel that he is one of us, especially after the trench work on individual training." Next time I shall write my own Platoon notes, but I had only just arrived when this lot were sent in.

I am reading now – at protracted intervals – a very delightful book called "Our Village" by Mary Russel Mitford. I strongly recommend it if you have not read it.

Kilroot Camp, Ulster
July 15th 1939

Thank you for your letter and sorry to be so long in answering it. As you see from my address I was suddenly whisked off to camp to be advance party. The Company arrives on Monday, and I am in sole charge with 32 men and now that we have nearly finished all preparations, having a nice time.

On July 12th no one was allowed out of camp, and it was practically besieged by the soldiers' girlfriends from Carrickfergus and Eden. The camp is delightfully situated about 16 miles from Belfast, and the sea is 200 ft from the Mess tent. I have two horses out here and ride daily which is very delightful. It is so nice to be away from stifling Belfast. The men seem to enjoy it; we pack up after lunch, and there is good bathing a short distance away – I haven't been in yet. We can see Scotland from here on a fine day. It is beautiful now – but we have just had nearly 12 hours rain. I shall really be sorry when the rest come out.

My course at Netheravon begins on the 8th, and I am applying to leave on Aug 4th, so I may get a couple of days at home. I can't see myself getting any leave after the course – but you never know.

July 25th 1939

We are having a delightful time in camp; There are Major Lane, Le Mesurier, Mayne, who is an RARO who hasn't done any soldiering since 1919, Boyne, Ormerod, and myself. We are out every day till about half past one, and after that there is nothing; we never go into Belfast but often into

Carrickfergus. We all went in last Friday in Lane's car for the annual pageant which began at 7.30 pm. By half past ten we were very thirsty, and by good luck I recognised a bobbie to whom I had given a lift in an army lorry about two months ago, when I was out reconnoitring. He immediately said that they never applied civil laws to the Military and sent a boy to find the pub owner: And so we all had a much needed glass of beer.

Tonight we go out on a night scheme, and on Friday we go out at 8 am and come back at 4 am on Saturday morning. I won't be able to leave Belfast until Saturday August 5th as we begin the company march on Thursday morning ending on the Saturday.

The first day of the march we do 24 miles to Crumlin, and then do a demonstration the next day at Lisburn which is 12 miles from Crumlin. On Saturday we do the final 12 miles to Belfast and that evening I shall catch a boat.

Out here the weather is glorious; I took a bathing parade the other day, and had my first dip – it was icy! Yesterday we had dinner out of doors, just Ormerod and myself, as the others were out, some on a Signal scheme, and one on pleasure. We drank to Admiral Rocks who captured Gibraltar 235 years ago; the Regiment was there.


In August, Richard attended a course at Netheravon. On September 2nd, Poland was invaded. Richard was on his way back to Belfast when he heard the news, on September 3rd, that war had been declared. He just had time to collect his belongings, before heading straight back to England.

August 14<sup>th</sup> 1939
Netheravon

We are having a very nice time here; and are comforted by the thought that there are no passing out exams: All the same work is quite strenuous, as on ordinary days we don't get off before 6.15 in the evening.

On Saturday three of us drove down to Bournemouth; I met a chap who had been at Brighton with me, who is now in the TA Gunners. I also saw Keith Goodall in the distance. Bournemouth has changed for the bad since we were there and I can't say I enjoyed going there much; it was at the height of the August holidays, and very hot. Salisbury is quite different; a delightful place – the Cathedral is marvellous.

I am probably playing cricket tomorrow afternoon – it will be a hot day I expect.


September 5<sup>th</sup> 1939
The Barracks, Chichester

Sorry not to have let you know before. I arrived Belfast 11 o'clock Sunday Morning, and seven hours later I left with a party for the Depot.[7] We crossed Larne-Stranraer and arrived at Portsmouth at half past eight last night and at the Depot about 10 o'clock, a pretty good journey.

# 3

## The Phoney War

The first months were known as the "phoney war" because nothing much seemed to happen. It did give Britain a chance to build up her armaments. Richard was involved in training, but even so much of life carried on quite normally with common concerns. Only one letter survives from this time, but there are three poems which reflect some of the fears and sorrows of the early months of the war.

### INTROSPECTION

I thought to see that burning orb
Sinking on the morrows mere
Now am I left with night alone
To die before the dawn is clear.

Death starts with life; life ends with death
Supreme he stalks our frightened race.
Today, Tomorrow, who can tell
When we will meet him face to face.

And now I know, for life is fast
Approaching sleeps tremendous sire
And soft remembrance sooths a soul
That once was fierce with strange desire.

October 26th 1939

# POLAND – AN ODE

The horsemen ride upon the West; the sky
Is black with smoke, and rent with hideous cry
The spectral Four are joined by yet another,
The Devil in a hun's disguise – their brother.
Eastwards they turn as blood red dawn appears
Striking their hearts with strange forboding fears.
The dawn is false, lit by a murderous hand
Deep dipped in shame, being a tyrant's brand
Hand of a snatcher from the grave – blood red-
From groping in the entrails of the dead.
The Hammer and the Sickle is the sign
Haunted on high by anti-Christian swine,
Grovelling, groping, crawling through the mire
They do their best to justify their hire
The Man of Steel is Man of Straw indeed
Forgoing all to satiate his greed.


Poland! Thy weeping children hold us yet
Nor from that bondage would we gladly fall.
The smoke of alien bombs thy funeral pall
The whine of shells speaks of the doom you net.
Upon thy side a mighty force is set
Forces of justice, Liberty, and Love
The might of right triumphant they will prove,
The time is done for foolish vain regret.
The story of thy martyrdom will live
And add to thine already noble past
A crown whose worth is dreamed by those who give
Their life's blood where the die of doom is cast.

O God of Battle help us as we strive
For victory to break the fiend at last.

"Poland is not yet dead" the warlike host
Of ancient Poland made the pious boast:
And echoing down the ages ran the theme
Which soon was fact; accomplished from the dream
Of all thy peoples. Poland all in all
Struggled against the dominating thrall,
Wherein was held by Russia's stern embrace
The freedom of a fierce and warlike race.
And part was held by Habsburgs double crown
Beneath whose rule a mighty race had grown.
And Prussian Frederick's heir was pleased to sway
His sceptre where a beaten people lay.
But when the war clouds gathered on apace
Poland was quick to seek her ancient place,
And from the ruins of the warring kings
She rose on high and spread her eagle wings.

Now as the night is dark and life is low,
Remember time is like the mighty sea
Though bound by fetters, yet forever free,
Continuous still with constant ebb and flow.
And Prussian force has struck a heavy blow
Combined with Austria her ancient sire
And Russia has not held her deadly fire
But brought to Poland misery and woe.
The tide of time will turn and as before
Those robbers will be humbled in the dust.
No man can read thy noble ageless love
But that he know th'inexorable must.

Poland, like Phoenix, rise again from fire
That proves to be aggression's funeral pyre.

November 7th 1939

## THE NEW YEAR

What will the new year bring? Methought I saw
A ghost in white crossing the strife – worn path;
The old year passing under a pall of snow
And following – the Infant year of war.

And now the year in his full short life has shown
Murder; for he has slain my own good friend
My mind is bitter and mournful at wanton slaughter
That leaves me – selfish in sorrow – alone.

Yes in spirit alone – and wistful as the moon
That weeps her silver radiance on the earth:
There stands alone in the paltry studded sky
Paging the laggard noon.

Why weep then; he has gone, and who has cared
I knew him. He lived and died it mattered not when
For time is long, and short, and is eternal,
And reeks not the serving hours of men.

January 1940?

The Drill Hall
Horsham January 28th 1940

Thank you very much for your letter which I should have answered earlier; however I have been very busy all the week and thought I would tell you all the news in one. On Tuesday we listened to the first of the official concert parties and they were extremely good – in fact it was the most enjoyable concert we have had since the outbreak; apparently they have been rottenly treated by some Regiments. They give a concert every night of the week; I should think it is very hard work.

That evening Patrick Bent asked me to be Best Man at his wedding on Friday, as the Adjutant had been attacked by 'flu and would be unable to perform – You can imagine that was an awful blow. On Thursday the Assistant Adjutant went down with 'flu, and I was hauled off at 7.30 in the morning to go with the Colonel on a Brigade TEWT near Maidstone – naturally I hadn't studied the scheme at all, still it was an interesting day – we didn't stop until five o'clock – and it was freezing the whole day – as we only had a few sandwiches at 12 o'clock we stopped for a reviver on the way home and it was very welcome.

I was terribly busy all Friday morning, but we got everything ready in time, and after lunch Patrick and I left for Haywards Heath where the wedding took place. The Colonel gave the bride away. I didn't lose the ring, and the reception went off very well. When everything was finished, and they had departed I, and two of the ushers, Walter Clarke, and Geoffrey Hodgson, went on to the Walters house near Bolney, as it was his 20th birthday. We had a very fine festive evening – I don't know how much we drank, but it was a considerable amount

– we got back somehow – I drove part of the way – it was great fun.

Luckily I was up early on Saturday morning, because Bartlett went off to Hospital for an operation – rather a serious one – and I am now commanding the new batch of Militia, a job which I am very glad to have, and I think they are going to be good. I have no other officers – for which I am thankful – but the best instructors in the Battalion.

In addition I am giving two lectures next week to all officers – and also lecturing my NCOs on Map Reading on Tuesday, and Section Leading on Friday – I give these lectures every week, even before I joined the Militia and am continuing them: They seem to be bearing some fruit; anyway it is good to have something to engage ones attention the whole time. The CSM of my company in the 2nd arrives here today to become R.S.M; I think he will shake them a bit.

Well, no more news, I am hoping to go to a Beethoven concert on Feb 10th, but I don't know yet. I will try for some leave a little later on, about the end of Feb, but at the minute I seem to be practically indispensable (says I) through illness, etc.

# 4

## France

In April 1940, the war stepped up a gear when Hitler attacked Norway. Richard left for France on April 21st, soon after his 21st birthday, as part of the British Expeditionary Force. He described to me the neat lines of white tents of their camp, and the terrifying sound of dive-bombers. But he did his best to make life comfortable, and many happy activities, such as cricket, continued. There are no letters from January to April, so by the next letter Richard is about to leave for France.

April 17th 1940

Dear Mummy and Daddy

Thank you both for your letters for my birthday, which passed off most successfully yesterday; I eventually got someone else to do my Orderly duties and was out by 7 pm, so we had a quiet but enjoyable party.

It will be no use writing to me after Thursday, but when you next do my address is

'B' Coy
6th Bn, The Royal Sussex Regiment
B. E. F.

I hear we get plenty of newspapers and things out there: the only thing I would really like is tobacco, and later on soap etc – 'tho it is really best to wait until we see the conditions under which we live. We are continuing our training out there so I suppose in due course we will achieve our ambition and become a first line unit. We will be under canvas which will be very nice – I hope!

I expect that by July nearly every country will be embroiled in the war – I don't appreciate Italy's[1] behaviour at all – I am sure the time is come for us to be thoroughly arrogant with refractory neutrals.

Well goodbye, pro tem; I will wire or phone before we go.


April 28th 1940  [France]


Thank you both for your letters which I received yesterday and the day before: all very welcome out here, as when we get properly settled there will be a post per diem . Well, we are getting on fine now – I think I told you I share a tent with  Walter, and we are making it as comfortable as possible; rush mats on the floor, tables, etc. My camp bed and mattress combined make a most comfortable bed, and I am the only officer in the Battalion with sheets – great forethought on my part. By the way, the remainder of the sheets and blankets are going to be sent on to you from the billet; they have the address, and will be laundered first. The rest of my stuff – i.e suitcase, dressing case, and hat box have gone to Walters home, as he popped over just before we went and took them with him.

Life has been fairly full here, and is going to be very much more so from tomorrow onwards. I will try and write a sort of diary letter, as the only time off will be after supper. I have explored the countryside with other subalterns, cementing the Entente! It is an historic part of the country, especially in our past History. Did you recall our conservation of some time ago when you read my last letter?

The worst thing here, taken all round is the food. The men's especially. What my platoon would appreciate most is cake – all sorts – if you ever send a parcel.

Well there really seems no news, other than that which I am unable to tell you. I spend a lot of time censoring the men's letters, and they all seem remarkably pleased with life which is a relief, but I've never known such prolific letter writers as some of them are!

Well no more now; I hope you are all well; and don't worry as we are far better off than ever we imagined.

April 28th 1940

Dear Daddy

Many thanks for your letter, which I got the day after Mummy's arrived – I must say we never expected the post to arrive as early as it did. I expect that, with memories of the last time, you would gasp at the luxury (comparative) in which we live. If it were not for the rain, which has turned everything into a quagmire, we would be very well off indeed.

It would be grand if you were living here, no petrol rationing, and whiskey 3 francs a glass, and wine 1 franc a glass.

I won 34 francs at Bridge last night which was pretty good. Thank you very much for the tenner; it will be very useful to me. I would love to have the Times weekly sent out, as the papers aren't as good as I thought at first, and it will give me all the news compactly.

May 2nd, 1940

We have been very busy recently – and beyond that I can tell you 'nowt' however I am thoroughly enjoying all that we are doing – we have something definite to achieve.

All my Platoon seem very happy under what must be very strange conditions to most of them. There is plenty of sport in the evenings or whenever we have time off. Soccer, boxing, and cricket. My chaps beat another team 5-1 at soccer the other day. Walter is going on a course in England shortly. He is very bucked about it. He and I have got a little Fox terrier, presented to us by a farm woman. She is called Follette and has been adopted by all the subalterns – in fact everyone is devoted to her. I hope Punch will not be too jealous.

At the minute a terrific thunder storm rages about our heads, and I write by the flickering light of a candle – a most pleasant olde worlde atmosphere!

An attempt was made to rob us of our Padre; but he fought a battle and is now back with us, thank goodness.

As I said in my last, cake and foodstuffs are most welcome as we have everything else in plenty

– I will write to Lalla and ask for an enormous Hunters Cake.


May 10th, 1940

Thank you so much for your letter, P.C., and cake which have just arrived: I have not yet tried the cake, but will let you know in my next what it is like; it looks very good.

We are terribly busy now; so please excuse a rather belated letter. We heard this morning of the latest example of Hun good taste! [2] I don't know what will happen now.


Sunday, May 12th, 1940

Hope you got my short letter alright. We have had a strenuous week, and the coming week holds promise of plenty of hard work.

Today we had an open air service in the morning and this afternoon we opened the cricket season. I got up a Company team against 'C' Company, and – mirabile dictu – I scored 16 runs and caught someone – no one was more surprised than myself, and no one else knows how near I was to dropping the damn thing!

The second parcel arrived yesterday – thank you very much for it. My chaps are going to have it tomorrow – I know they will love it.

I enclose two souvenir cards which will amuse you and Daddy I should think. All the men are sending them home, so I thought I would follow suit. I also include a 'souvenir' which was proudly presented to me by a small boy who assured me it was 'all his own work'!

The weather has been wonderful here; I am so brown you would hardly recognise me. Two evenings ago I played soccer for the Officers v the Sergeants – they put me in goal, and the Sergeants won 5-0. Still as I have not played since I was twelve it wasn't too bad.

I think the Germans have really made a bad move this time – most tactless of them – and it shows that besides having no manners at all they are bullies and cowards.

Well, the general feeling of laziness bids me lay down my pen. I quote "The moan of doves in immemorial elms, and murmuring of innumerable bees" which, except that there are few elms, and no bees, describes the afternoon very well.

The German army, under Rommel, had attacked through the Ardennes using blitzkrieg tactics, advancing rapidly on a narrow front. They managed to drive a line between the British and the French forces, and to reach the coast near Boulogne. A large part of the British Expeditionary Force was left surrounded by German troops. On May 26th the BEF was authorised to leave via Dunkirk, and Operation Dynamo took place between May 27th and June 1st. 338,226 allied soldiers were taken from the beaches of Dunkirk back to England. Of these, 123,095 were French. Many Royal Sussex men from the 2nd Battalion were taken prisoner, and remained in Germany throughout the war.

But there were still 150,000 British troops left in France, also many Poles and Canadians. Many ships sailed from England to rescue troops from ports along the Channel and along the West Coast. Richard and the 6th Battalion of the Royal Sussex Regiment were rescued by one of these. They had been bombarded at Amiens, but managed to commandeer a train and travel Westwards. Richard had been on a train driving course and drove the train part of the way. They also did a lot of marching, and ended up at Blain near Nantes. The next letters were written as they were waiting for transport back to England.

May 24th, 1940  [near Nantes, France]

Well here at last is the letter I've been hoping to write for over a week. I don't know whether you have any Field Service Pcs but you ought to have had two by now.

Anyway don't worry again if you ever have a long lapse like that, it is only because it has been absolutely impossible to write owing to circumstances beyond our control. As a matter of fact we have just finished a rather energetic period, but are now back resting and reorganising. It is lovely here, you can't imagine what good food, water to wash in, and a good nights rest meant to us last night. There is also a river in which I have already bathed – Delicious! By the way I have received no letters or papers or anything from anyone at all for about 10 days or more. I expect they have been caught in the Hun advance on the coast. I'm so glad Moseley is in jug, and very grieved to hear that England is now completely Nationalised. Still I suppose it's win or lose all.

Now remember we are in a wonderful place well away from anything and likely to remain here for a little time, so on no account get worried. I will write to everyone when I get time.

May 30th, 1940

Many thanks for your letter dated May 15th which we received the day before yesterday. I'm afraid that we will never receive a lot of the subsequent mail as the God of War has ordained that it fall into other hands than ours; so if you have written since, please recount anything important. I'm so glad you got the souvenirs; I will send some more as opportunity serves. We are having a very quiet time now and thankful for it while it lasts – not for long I'm afraid. One of my feet is causing me considerable annoyance at the moment as the result of the last two weeks but it will soon go off. The Colonel is suffering from gout; I went up and saw him the other day; he is very cheerful all things considered. I received a parcel from Lalla by the same post as yours; very lucky it arrived at all. I hope everyone is well and that you are enjoying the same beautiful weather as we are.

The Belgian debâcle has given me a shock; the newspapers here refer to him as 'Le roi felon' [3]who has betrayed his Father, his people, and his allies; I could never have thought it possible. Still we are all very confident, the French especially so.

Well, there seems little news that can be penned, 'tho I could write for hours if there were no restrictions. All my chaps are well and in the best of spirits, and I have scrounged a complete set of cricket gear from the R.A.O.C and we play most evenings.

Saturday June 8th 1940

Well, to date I have received only two letters one from you and one from Daddy both written about the middle of May; but nothing since. However yesterday I got one from Aunt G dated May 31st which wasn't too bad, in answer to a Field P.C. of mine. I have heard very bad news of our poor 2nd Battalion.[4] I only hope it isn't true. There is so very little news; we are working like hell our day begins at quarter to six and we stop work at 5.30 or 8 in the evening, working all the week Sundays included. At the time of writing I have just been moved again and am on a special and more pleasant job however even in this I was up at quarter to five this morning. We bathe every day now in a very pleasant canal which joins a certain very large river in Western France.

I may have the chance to tell you everything much sooner than we think!

The eleventh day of June in this year of disgrace 1940.

Half an hour after I posted my last letter I received yours dated May 31st so now the mail is coming through alright. Last night we heard of the Fascist act. So Italy has sold herself again.[5] I wonder what the price is that Hitler offered – who knows, perhaps Egypt. I should love to have a crack at the icescreamers – frankly I should prefer them to a hun, but I suppose we cannot be choosers.

We have had the most unexampled spell of good weather which looks as if it is beginning to break just now. The temperature must have been well over 80 for the last fortnight. These last four days I have been extremely slack in fact I can say I've had my summer holiday – wish it could have been at home. I look forward with interest to see who is going to take the rap for the colossal muddle of these last few weeks. I hope someone gets it in the neck. I have been talking to the Colonel of Michael Wilkes' Battalion: I hear that Michael was left at home with other details, just as we left some of ours: So he is safe. Jack Beckwith hasn't joined us yet, I hear he is still at Worthing waiting to come out. I don't suppose he ever will. I am still separated from my men, 'tho I went over and saw them yesterday and they were all very well and quite happy.

[Diary entries from small 1940 diary:-]

*April 21st  Leave Horsham and Southampton*

*April 22nd  Arrive Le Havre; arrive Abancourt*

*May 9th  Holland and Belgium invaded*

*May 17th  Prepare to leave A(bancourt)  Now we are really going to do something, perhaps!*

*May 18th  En route through Amiens.  Big German air raid. 10 killed, 40 wounded.*

*May 19th  Defensive position at Ailly.  Bombardment of Amiens.*

*May 20th  Move up to wood.  Get away by night. Germans 6 miles away*

*May 21st  Reach Achine (?)[Achere]*

*May 22nd  Leave Achine  [Achere]*

*May 23rd  Reach Blain [near Nantes]  Chateau Pont Pietin.*

*June 10th  Italy declares war – Toolooralay*

*June 15th  Canoeing in morning.  Leave Pont Pietin for Savernay*

*June 16th  Leave Savernay for St Nazaire.  Whole BEF on road.*

The above entries cover part of the missing period between May 12th and May 24th.

Richard and his platoon boarded "The City of Mobile" at St Nazaire. Shortly before, the Lancastria had been bombed in the harbour with the loss of over 3000 men. It was the greatest single Naval disaster of the war, and only a mile from "The City of Mobile". Even nearer was the "Florestan", on which some of the Battalion also escaped, and the third ship which rescued them was the "Glenaffric".

# 5

## Saving England

The "City of Mobile" had some difficulty getting in to England. All the South coast ports were blocked. Eventually they landed at Southampton, and were sent to Northampton. From there Richard and his platoon were billeted in Northumberland. And then began the long frustrating three and a half years' wait for a posting overseas.

When Richard talked about these times, he portrayed them as idle. But reading the letters it is clear they were very busy. There were route marches, battle schools, periods of building defences and defending the coast. The letters also show the muddle of war – the last minute changes, the reorganisations, the continual relocations.

No 1 Gunnerton Camp
Wark
Nt Hexham
Northumberland

June 24th 1940

Just a line to give you my full address which is as above. As you gathered we arrived at Southampton from St Nazaire – The journey took us four and half days. Still I will tell you all about that when I come on leave. My Platoon and I finally located the Battalion up here and we have all got back except one officer and a few men and we hope they managed alright. We are fifteen miles from the nearest town – very bleak country and of course. I have neither my sleeping bag nor my lilo – there is just a chance that they were conveyed to England, 'tho I'm not very hopeful – still I refrain from buying too much until I know when I get leave. I shall have forty eight hours, and two days thrown in for travelling – not very much I'm afraid.

There are no letters from June 24th 1940 to January 8th 1941. It was during these months that they were in Dunstable and Luton, guarding ball bearing and transport works. The following poems date from that time.


## LINES WRITTEN IN DISGUST AT LUTON

Luton
Has no Bruton
Street
Where one may meet
Pleasant people, walking, walking
Up and down and talking, talking
Rot, to others even more elite.

No!
Luton workers
Are not shirkers:
How they work, poor dears, and so
When the blasted sirens blow
Luton workers flock below
To some subterranean spot
Not, oh reader, mark you, not

To save themselves – Oh dear me . No!
For if some damn great bomb should blot
Them out, then who could stop the rot
And save the country in its peril
Twixt the deep blue sea and devil,
Meaning Hitler! By the way,
Who would draw their whacking pay:
Certainly not they, and so
Luton workers down you go.

October 6th 1940


## ON GOING INTO WINTER QUARTERS IN DUNSTABLE

Lift Dunstable your dreaming spires
And all your ugly chimney stacks
Lay on your long-neglected lyres –
The Army's marching in – in slacks!

Wake not to bugle or to drums
Nor hope to see the standards flutter
Hark, hark! The Motor Transport comes
And carrions stentorian stutter.

The Saxon Way, the Roman Road
Have changed since last you closed your eyes
Our warriors wear no longer woad,
And he is old, who never dies.
Soldiers: the first since Caesars time,
Will stay and make your town their home;

Good Heavens! Here's a Roman dime,
Lets hope all roads still lead to Rome.

November 11th 1940

THE WORKERS SONG

This is the song of the workers
This is the song of their toil
This is the song of their wages
They've been singing it for ages
(And what a cacophony)
Of their progress from the soil.
Happy soil!
It's written in Red Revolution
It's written in strikes in war
It's written by men
(Pardon the word)
With virulent pen
Who know when
To keep in with the law.

For every man has a conscience
Which may not permit him to fight,
Except in the cause
Of his own bloody laws
Up wrong, and down with the right.
For we're starved and kept down
By that tyrant frown.
No money – well, hardly any
And certainly not a penny
When we've had all our beer
To spend on the wife's new gown.

The working classes must be freer
So down with the swine
Who send our comrades up the line –
Of course we would be there if we could
But the manager begged us to stay –
And we'll have his place one day.
Then we'll have to forget those fine
Fellows who fought for us in the line;
For the missus wants to be Lady Shunk,
I don't care myself (ha ha), but still I funk
Her more
Than ever I funked the war.


70th Bn. The Royal Sussex Regt.
Chichester

January 8th 1941


I regret that in future my letters must be addressed RGS Tolson Esq. In other words, my 'pip' has gone with the wind, as I thought it would. However do not be distressed, I will get it back soon, I have no doubt.

Today we went on a very long Battalion route march, strenuous and tiring, especially for me. We started at 9 o'clock and got back at 3.30 pm. Apparently several of my brother officers did not expect me to finish it owing to my illness, I don't know why they should think this. I have many old acquaintances here, and the regimental feeling is delightful and gratifying after the luke warm atmosphere of the 6th.

I have a new batman a very nice fellow by the name of Fisher very willing and helpful, although new to the game.

Alas! we are leaving dear Chichester for Bexhill very shortly; I will keep you posted, I don't know the date yet! Very tired tonight. No more now.

The next letters come from the East coast, which they had been sent to defend. It was thought quite possible that there would be an invasion in April 1941. Work preparing trenches and laying wire was almost continuous, until a day came in summer when it was decreed that Sunday could be a rest day. Richard always spoke of Suffolk, especially Covehithe, with great affection, although it doesn't always show in the letters.

Suffolk
1941 [Summer – undated]

Thank you for you last letter; sorry to have delayed in answering. I have just returned from a conference, which I hope is the last I shall hear about the exercise I mentioned, and which I expect you read about in the papers. Actually it was quite good fun, 'tho pretty tough for the men in parts. It was boiling hot, especially the day we marched to Norwich – we were supposed to be Mobile Troops! – and I got very sun burned; as usual the whole organisation was a delightful muddle, and even after attending the conference I can't understand why the High Command took some of the decisions they did. Still our chaps were very good, and probably learned a bit.

I am going on a two day Messing Course this week at Bury St. Edmunds – should be quite useful, and then we have a Battalion TEWT to finish the week.

We are bathing in the sea quite regularly now, tho I have not been in myself – I suppose I ought to one of these days.

Royal Norfolk & Suffolk Yacht Club
Lowestoft

August 17th 1941

Dear Daddy

Just a line to tell you no news at all. I hope you had a pleasant journey back after John's party in Town. I have not heard from him since, tho' he said he would write.

The latest rumours are that we stay here all the winter – I hope that they will not come true.

I have become a member (temporary) of this club; it is the only place in Lowestoft where one can get anything to eat – or drink! I have been commanding the Company for the last week, and been on the range twice – the standard of shooting is appalling – much worse than when we left for France.

I have had yet another letter from Walter – he has now joined the 1st Battalion, and seems to be having a good time in Cairo. I wish I could join him.

# AUTUMN – UNFINISHED MUSINGS

The first fell falling leaves of Autumn, brown
And azure bronze, flee unresisting down;
Unclothing weald, wold, but wearing yet
A richer crown than worn by Bajazet.
Decay foretells the coming of December –
But you remember life, and know not death, September.

September in Suffolk –
O rare delight, and almost holy –
Suffolk folk are wholly holy
Summer had come to England and passed Suffolk by.

Summer in September
September in Suffolk
We will remember that crowning moment
We will remember God's grace anew.
I know now, and you know, but how few
Others know.

Miracle! Wonderful! –
How summers ebb and flow.
Spirit of time and tide
Surely it has defied
Some winter when it wills – we are rewarded
Faith renewed has been accorded
Faith that will never be denied.

September 1941

Battle H.Q. [Suffolk]
The Royal Sussex Regiment
October 2nd 1941

Thank you for your letter to hand yesterday. I was beginning to wonder whether you had received mine as I gave it to one of the men to post. As you see I am in my Company Battle HQ, have been since Monday – and will be until Saturday. I am commanding in Upton's absence, and quite enjoying myself. But I shall be very glad to have a normal nights rest on Saturday. Your note and newspaper cutting have just arrived – it is very interesting. I had no idea that anyone ventured to criticize the army so strongly as this fellow.

It is exceedingly cold at night now, but luckily very fine. All the men live and cook, eat and sleep in the trenches, and so far I'm glad to say they seem to be enjoying it.

Halesworth
Suffolk
Sunday November 2nd 1941

Thank you for your letter, and glad you had an uneventful trip back. Have delayed writing in order to make this a birthday letter. Many Happy Returns of the Day.

Jack Beckwith is going on a Company Commanders course on the 12th and I am taking over 'A' Company for five weeks, and am going there on this Tuesday to learn my way about. It should be quite amusing, and a change from being 2 in command.

We are comfortably settled in here, very comfortably; a furnished cottage, bath etc, and a gas fire in my bed room, which without it would be as cold as charity as it faces North East.

I shall really be quite sorry to leave this little house – but no doubt I shall make myself comfortable with 'A'. All letters in future A Company please.

I have had a very full week. An all day scheme the day after I arrived back, a 23 mile route march on Wednesday on which I took the Company – very stiff afterward but no sore feet; it snowed and hailed continuously from about 9 o'clock until 1.30 so we all got thoroughly wet through and it was blisteringly cold! The Company Commander deigned to come out with the hot tea and march the remaining 10 miles; good show, what!

It is, I believe quite unusual to have snow at this time of year up here, and so far we have had no more – but it rains every day and nearly every hour.

On Friday we were up at 5.30 in the morning and went to Bury St Edmunds for a big demonstration of the Attack. Chaps from all over the country came to it. Very good but oh! so cold in a coach with no windows. Happy birthday once more, and I shall try and get a week end near to Christmas – probably just afterwards.

November 20th 1941
[Suffolk]

The only reason I can get for my abrupt non departure is that suddenly no more officers of my category are needed; but that is as much as anyone knows, so I can push it no further.

I am back in the old place in C Company – I am glad to say I have not gone to 'A' – for many reasons.

From now on my address is 'C' Company, the R Sx Regt, Maidenhead, Berks. Is that a surprise? Well I wasn't far out in my prognostication though I had no idea the move would be so immediate. We leave here Saturday, spend the night at a camp not far from our last station, and land up in the Royal County Sunday afternoon. It should be pleasant – at any rate by comparison, and it is very near home which is a fine thing – but oh! how I pine for the Nilgiris – if that is how they are spelt! It is really for the change rather than an actual desire to go to India – 'tho probably it would be out of the Frying Pan!

The day after I got back I received two beautiful pipes in a case – a present from two of my men in B Company; they had heard I was going away. It is that sort of thing that makes one feel life is worth while – if you know what I mean – that one is not entirely forgotten – or am I being egotistical?

Maidenhead Berks
November 29th 1941

Thank you for yours, and sorry to be so late in answering. We have had an energetic week but are now settled in.

We left Southwold on Saturday morning, our convoy was 9 miles long and took 25 minutes to pass any given spot. As usual all the arrangements for the actual journey were appalling, and we arrived at Knebworth in pitch darkness instead of at about 4.30 in the afternoon. There we stayed the night in tents in a wood, with no guides to show us to the tents, the chaos of a whole Battalion in those woods was incredible. I slept or tried to sleep, that night on the muddy floor of the tent, wrapped in my great coat and gas cape – my men did have two blankets which I made them take from the coach, but even they were not much help – and of course it rained all night! We went on our way at nine next morning, arriving at Taplow at about 1 o'clock.

We are actually in Buckinghamshire, at Springfield House Taplow – a very large and pleasant house that accomodates all the Company and two officers, myself and the Company Commander. I have a nice bedroom, with running water, and a bathroom next door – what a change from Covehithe!

# 6

## Further Training

There were two personal sorrows during the next years. Richard's brother John, a pilot in Bomber Command, was killed when his plane crashed in Northern Ireland in March 1942. A little more than a year later his father died at the age of 57. As mentioned earlier, he also was a Regular soldier, who had survived the First World War, and the Battle of the Somme, where he was badly wounded. In WWII he joined the RAF and was managing three RAF stations when he died. It was a gruelling job. These deaths were of course extremely sad for Richard and his brother David, and especially for their mother.

The long wait for an overseas posting continued. The next letter comes from Bexhill, which is perhaps where the following poems were written.


**WHY WAS I FIGHTING?**

They asked me why I was fighting –
Well, what could I really say?
I could rhapsodise on the nightin-
Gale and the dawn of day
I could fight like a myriad newsmen
For learning – Equality – Rot!
But I don't think then, I could tell when
I knew I had gained the lot.
And what is there left to fight for
When you cut out all the aforesaid?

The right to ask for a little more,
And to make, and lie, on your own bed!

Added in pencil:

The Englishman's creed

Domine dirige nos
O Lord direct us in thy path,
That we may never tell a lie
And every evening take our bath.

24th January 1942


## MY VERY DEAR FRIEND
*A letter written to* Walter Stevenson Clarke Esqre

Do you miss England Walter? Then
England must miss you too.
But there are many changes, and
I'll tell you of a few.
The homes so old and stately
Are mostly up for sale,
And the rustic humble cottage
Would bow down before a gale.
The village green at eventide
Echoes no childish play –
The Transports legacy of mud
Has mashed its green to grey.

The fragrant English garden
Is fraught with turnip tops
And the fulsome English countryside
Is ploughed and tilled by Wops.
That wood alive with Springes now
And Spring when it arrives,
Will find those cruel Springes still,
For on their crop man thrives.

Each city street and city square
Are broken up with tons
Of German frightfulness, and now
Are city polygons.
The uplands and the downlands
The country you love best –
Yes England knows you cherish her
She waits at your behest.

Yes, England knows you miss her, yes
And England bids you care
For those who face the boredom
And the blackout over here.

We speak as a great people
We the gaunt grey hills of Wales;
We the stripling streams that sing
Along the timeless English dales.
We the black peat bogs of Ulster,
We the purple Scottish crags
We the whale-back downs of Sussex;
We the Berkeley Bar and Quags! [1]

We are with you, are you with us?
We are brothers, cry it loud –
And the earth will know our thunder
And the tyrant's head is bowed.

February 1942

## TO SIR SAMUEL HOARE

"Methinks he doth protest too much"

Shall Chelsea boast – Munchausen is the name
Even Laval could scarce endure such shame.
Shades of Carlyle – His lusty shade would roar
"Castles in Spain". "Tis pity he's a Hoare".[2]

## SOLDIER FRIENDS

| | |
|---|---|
| Patrick Bent to his work | Patrick Bent |
| With a will! | Married Feb 1940 |
| He didn't shirk | |
| Or lurk – | |
| Or sleep his fill! | |
| He worked so fast | |
| The last | |
| We heard | |
| He'd got the bird! | |

| | |
|---|---|
| My name is Ball | Major Ball RAMC |
| I do not bat | |
| An eye at that! | |
| The joke, if joke at all | |
| Is flat. | |

Freddie was a gent!  Fred Maxse, Captain
He never joked at Major Ball
Or Mr Bent
But – taken all in all –
He's heaven sent.

As pants the mouse for piece of cheese  Rev' d ARC Leaney,
When first he smells the bait –  a remark from the pulpit
So long I for his blood,
Who put a button in the plate!

The Padre
Went on an N.C.O.'s Cadre.
He lost his stripe
For talking the most abominable tripe.

I'm the Colonel  E.K.B. Wannop
Stop this infolonel  Lt. Colonel
Noise
You boys!

Parker  Doug Parker, 2nd Lt.
Was right marker  Killed 1941
Of the Bn.
What a stn.
Freddie Maxse
Grew intolerably waxy.
He said imperiously
You really must take me seriously!

Bexhill
February 12th 1942

We have been exceptionally busy since I came back – only 3 officers pro tem. I landed into another long route march on the Thursday and of course it snowed the whole way except for the last four miles. Still it was a good marching temperature. Every evening too we are engaged on out-of-hours work – chiefly enlarging maps, descriptions of cross-country marches, and other trivialities; nevertheless they have kept me in every evening since I've been back; often working until 10 pm: However I am determined to go to the cinema tomorrow evening to see 'The Great Lie' with Bette Davis in it.

On Tuesday and Wednesday there was a big defence exercise; I was an Umpire, as our recruit Company did not take part. We were right on the edge of England, and dawn on Wednesday was wonderful to see, the first time I've been out at dawn for some considerable time. The exercise went off fairly well – luckily the days and the night were the best we could expect for the time of year, and it was not cold – a very different contrast from this morning. Today, of course, we've had conferences and post mortems, all very tedious – and an excellent leafier on battle drill from a Canadian Officer in the Calgary Highlanders.

I saw the other day that Dick English has been presented with a son; and today that Audrey Lynam[3] has had a baby – Hum will be pleased!

Spring 1942, Bexhill

I have just finished reading a remarkable book, 'After Many A Summer' by Aldous Huxley – a novel in cynical and scintillating style, a compound of theosophy and metaphysics and satire, with a terrific 'twist' at the end. Well worth reading. I had no idea he was so easy to read.

This last week has been quiet and cold and it snowed yesterday and this morning, which is a pity after the promise of Spring at the beginning of the week. I refereed a Soccer match on Wednesday, just a Company one, having read up the rules of Soccer just before the game began. It was quite good fun and I wasn't chased off the field which was very gratifying.

There really seems to have been no news this week. I am doing a short Mortar Course beginning Tuesday until Friday – it is just a local show.

C/o GPO Gravesend, Kent
April 15th 1942

Dear Daddy

I am still on my battle drill and thoroughly enjoying it, now that I have got over my initial stiffness! We had a whole day out yesterday and arrived home dripping wet having waded through two different streams, covered about 16 miles and done several schemes on the march. It is certainly good training. I don't know whether I will get my weeks leave now when I hoped owing to taking charge of battle drill training in my Company when I return next week – but I may, and if I don't I shall put in for a week end over the 25th, getting home on the Friday evening.

Kent
May 10th 1942
Thank you muchly for yours which arrived Saturday afternoon. Very glad David doing so well

in his tests. He is evidently a military genius, like his brother!

Well, I have had a very hard but none the less enjoyable week training two Platoons of the Company, and next week I have the remaining two to put through it. It has been so warm that on two occasions I have taken them swimming in Gravesend Open Air baths, and even gone in myself, which is pretty good considering I didn't bathe once last year. We may be going on this scheme on Thursday, 'tho no definite news yet – we march to Horsham of all places, spend a day or two round there, and then march and fight to D-V-R, and then home via C-N-U-B-R – [4] where I shall enjoy seeing the Cathedral. Then in June we are training with the Home Guard at Godalming – not Bordon.

My new uniform has just arrived and is not at all bad; I think I shall bring it home when I get 48hrs leave.

I am writing, at the express request of the 2nd in Command, some trifles for the Regimental Magazine. One is the Company Notes – the second is a poem entitled "On hearing the first Cuckoo on Company Training", and the third is a short story. I don't suppose any of them will be accepted.

Sunday 17th May 1942

[Kent]

Thank you for yours and Tubby's [5]enclosed. Very nice of him to write; I didn't imagine for one minute that his soeur would remember my call, let alone my name.

Well, I have been away all this weekend umpiring the big scheme at 'Guildford' which I expect you have read about in the papers. We left here by train on Saturday morning and I had lunch in Guildford with Mrs Prescott and Martin who were there. Then a very dreary and completely confusing conference at which it turned out that they did'nt intend to feed us and certainly hadn't a bed for us that night. Well, I and two other officers who were umpiring the Canadian Tanks drove all over the countryside and eventually, and unaided, found them – by then it was 8.15 pm and we were very hungry.

Luckily I discovered that there was a very large sort of Country Hotel a mile down the road. We got an extraordinarily good, and cheap meal, and having made love to the proprietress she let us sleep in the cocktail bar – one sofa for each of us, and gave us tea and biscuits at 0500 hrs in the very early morning. So we were very lucky, were we not. Nothing to pay for our couches, and heaven knows what we would have done in the open with no coats or blankets between us.

I rode in a tank the whole way and had great fun, especially after we got into Guildford and streaked up and down the High Street with syren wailing and throwing thunder flashes and smoke bombs.

The Canadians were an exceedingly nice lot – the pleasantest I've met yet. Owing to good work by the Tanks the scheme was over earlier than expected. We got up to London for lunch at 2 pm, saw a News flick and came back here.

I feel quite weary, as I was training hard all last week, and only knew about the scheme at 7 o'clock on Friday. We leave on our big scheme very shortly, and I may not receive your letters as we have no postal address but I will keep you well posted from my end.

A from 'A'Coy70<sup>th</sup> R Sussex Regt.
c/o GPO, Bordon, Hants.
[undated]   [June 1942]

Just a line to say that we have arrived here, and are off to Godalming today. But the address is as above. We have marched 62 miles in two days and finished the journey by Transport yesterday. We spent last night under canvas behind Broxhead house. We went over to Godalming yesterday evening and we are very nicely situated. I shall be able to get 24hrs clear any day next week. Can you make town, or don't you think its worth it just for the day. If you can, I suggest Tuesday Wednesday, or Thursday. I can be up by lunch time.

c/o GPO Margate, Kent
A.D. Quint. Ides. Jul.

I'm acting Company Commander and enjoying a brief spell of authority. My leave is O.K. I'll be with you on Monday next some time in the afternoon. We have a Brigadiers inspection tomorrow: he's going to watch us bathing I believe.

We saw some Jerries over here the other evening, but they were not interested in this cultured Seaside resort.

For the first time for many weeks I've read two decent books. "I, Claudius", which you've probably read, and which I thought delightful, and "The Sword in the Scabbard" by Michael Joseph, the publisher; about the army in England for the year following Dunkirque. Very interesting and true.

We are loosing a good many men now to service Battalions. What do you think of that?

Ante Diem tertium Kalendas Aug. MCMXLII
[Kent]

Safely arrived, after visiting Jones in London and a snack at the 'Criterion'; I got there very early before anyone else was thinking of eating, but it filled up rapidly. I was greeted with the news that we were moving the next day, and monstrous early at that – however as a concession to my leave-weary self, they allowed me to bring the Company transport down and so I had a pleasant enough journey, some seventeen miles or so.

We are now in the Kent of my imagination – the real Garden of England. A tiny village called Goodnestone – situate half way between Canterbury and Sandwich, with, I should imagine, not more than 200 inhabitants. We are in the grounds of Goodnestone House – magnificently Georgean – but now deserted. We live in Nissen huts. And train vigorously all day. The weather is now at its best. Yesterday evening I fielded a cricket eleven of our not so goods against the Artillery, and had an enjoyable game, altho' we were severely beaten. I umpired in order to watch the 'form'. We are going to play again with our real team on Sunday or Tuesday, and hope to show them what's what.

August 14th 1942 [Margate]

We have left Goodnestone with many regrets and are now up at Margate – or rather Cliftonville, which is nicer. I have suddenly become Battalion Sports Officer for a short time, and played yesterday; we beat the Civil Defence team satisfactorily, 'tho I made a duck. I am trying to arrange an inter-company knock out competition, which should prove exciting.

Bathing is now prohibited for all and sundry, which is rather a blow; quite a number of our fellows have learned to swim since we have been here.

43rd Div School Home Forces
August 25th 1942

Sorry to have been so long writing, but I was suddenly sent on a Battle Course, and until this evening we have literally not had one hour to ourselves.

The last effort I was on was child's play compared to this – for one thing we never stop running – 1 hour for lunch – ¾ of an hour for tea, probably a lecture after tea – not tonight however, then supper, and a film of some description, training, etc, after dinner. I can tell you I'm jolly glad to get to bed at 9.30. But its great fun – at any rate in retrospect, and the instructors are good chaps. We fire all weapons, even German and Italian rifles. Yesterday a Hun plane paid us a surprise visit but not for long – I'm not allowed to say where we are, for security reasons – but I hope for a weekend when this is over. Tomorrow we have a 'night-op' to add to the horrors.

We have a very comfortable Mess here, and need it, and the food is not bad. Also I have my batman with me which is a blessing – but not for him, as they give them plenty of work and training too.

September 3rd 1942 [Battle School]

Dear Daddy

Many Happy Returns of the Day; I hope you had a pleasant party with Mummy and David over the week end. Wish I could have managed some leave, but I've waited until the last minute, and still had no reply from Battalion, 'tho I wrote last week.

The course is nearly finished, and I return to Margate on Saturday; It has been pretty hard going all the time, and tomorrow we have a final all day bust up, with no food between breakfast and Dinner. However it is the last day, and so won't seem so bad.

I hear that our Battalion had changed its role again since I have been away – no doubt for the worse. I seem to make no headway at all in the Battalion, and I do dearly want to do something. I suppose its no use asking Uncle B[6] again, but it's a pretty miserable outlook and I shall try and get a transfer when I get back. The danger is that one might be sent to something worse like the 30th Battalion. But it is very worrying and humiliating.

September 20th 1942 [Margate]

I am very busy, and tomorrow shall be distilling some of my recently acquired knowledge to an NCOs Cadre. I have been selected to attend a two day course on speaking to the men and keeping them informed on political and Current Affairs generally. This is on Oct 6th, and should be quite interesting.

September 27ᵗʰ 1942
[Caterham]

Dear Daddy
Well here we are in the heart of Surrey which I prefer infinitely to the Kentish Coast. Sorry not to have answered yours earlier; I wrote a letter last Sunday, and then tore it up; I find the question of the future very difficult to give a definite answer on. I did quite well on my battle course, and I gather that the 2 in command here thinks fairly well of my work, and it seems as if I might possibly get my rank back, and if I go somewhere else it will mean the spade work all over again. On the other hand I don't want to spend another summer here, especially as I think – with big things brewing. So you see I'm in a bit of a quandary – what ever happens I want to get going actively next year. Can you advise me. I don't want the Middle East now, I think Europe will get its whack next year.

The Royal Sussex Regiment
Margate
Kent
Written this Sunday, the One Hundred and Eighty Third Anniversary of the Glorious Victory over the French at Quebec [7]

I hope you had an enjoyable time down at Andover. I had a letter from Daddy saying that you had all had a good stay. Sorry I couldn't get down, but Battalion took no notice of my plea for leave. We are leaving here shortly and proceeding to a place much nearer home, so I think I will hold over for three weeks or so now.

The Course was great fun and has made me very fit. I think I did fairly well. I must finish now or I shall miss another post.

c/o GPO Godalming Surrey
The Eve of Waterloo [8]

'There was a sound of revelry by night' ... but in our case it is only caused by training the Home Guard. Tonight we go to Charterhouse to put them through a spot of battle discipline. Last night I was the author of a small scheme in which three Platoons of the HG participated, and it was quite successful ending at about a quarter past ten. They are still remarkably keen here and turn up every night. Last Saturday and Sunday we had full days with them – in fact we are working quite hard, and enjoying it. All the HG Platoon Commanders are pleased with the show and are very hospitable; we have tea with one, baths, and today two of us went to lunch with the Company Commander. He is trying to get us down again later in the year.

Caterham Surrey
October 22nd 1942

Sorry to have been so many days in answering. Work pressure tremendous, and very tiring. In addition I am practicing for the Battalion rugger XV. I still have to do all the outdoor work for our tests on Nov 2nd, 3rd and 4th, and in addition the work of 2 in command, Administration Officer, and run the Company Canteen. You can imagine I feel dog tired at nights, especially after a very strenuous march, as we had today.

Caterham
December 6<sup>th</sup>, 1942

Did you see the notice of the funeral at Chichester,[9] I attended it with the acting C.O and one other officer, representing this Battalion. We travelled down by train. The slow march through Chichester with the Regimental band playing the funeral march was very impressive, but I did not like the service in the Cathedral – something lacking. I met a lot of old friends there, including Bob Penney, and Arnold Bartlett. Arnold is a captain at the I.T.C. Colchester, and hates it. Bob Penney was his usual delightful self, 'tho he has also lost his Majority. We lunched at the Dolphin and Anchor, which was crowded out by the Regiment. They could not put us up at the depot, no room, 'tho I managed to have a talk with 'Egg' Ashworth, who is commanding there.

# 7

## At Last!

Richard continued to be disappointed for the first half of 1943, but towards the end of the year he got his wish and was posted abroad. By 1942, the war was being fought on several fronts. Hitler made the great mistake of invading Russia in June 1941. Japan attacked Pearl Harbour in December bringing the United States of America into the war, and before the end of 1941 Hong Kong had fallen to the Japanese. Other British territories were to follow. The European war was being fought in North Africa, where the German General Rommel had great success. But in November 1942 the Germans were defeated at El Alamein, and other allied victories in the desert followed.

In July 1943 the Allies invaded Italy, starting with the island of Sicily. Their aim partly was to involve German troops, drawing them away from the Russian front and a future front in Northern Europe.

Sunday [February 7th 1943]          Caterham

Infuriated, but resigned to the blows of fate, I just hope I shall be able to get leave very shortly, possibly after the fifth of the month. It seems to be my misfortune now to have my leave put back at the crucial moment. More men going and several officers already gone, one of them to my old mob, but I don't want to go back to them. The only chaps still left there are the ones I disliked.

We are having a last route march on Wednesday. I have had to select the route – it should be quite good fun, 18¼ miles.

One of our chaps has just been killed in a motor cycle accident this morning, poor fellow. I don't know whose fault it was that the accident occurred.

Well no more now, even Sunday I have work to do!? Terrible isn't it.

Small Arms School
Hythe Wing, Bisley Camp
Brookwood Surrey

February 24th 1943

Dear Daddy

Many thanks for your letter. We have been through so much turmoil in the last week that I thought I would delay writing until I knew what was going to happen.

Anyway I am now on a five weeks course at Bisley, and I think it is going to be very enjoyable and interesting: I've always wanted to go, and the C.O. fixed it for me at very short notice – in fact I did'nt know for certain until Monday morning.

Eight of our officers are on embarkation leave – but they are not on a very good thing, so I'm glad I wasn't sent.

I think I should get my Captaincy fairly soon as I seem to be in the COs good books at the minute. He was saying the other day how well he remembered you, and talking about the 3rd Battalion dinners. However, he's so changeable that I shall probably incur his disfavour before long. I shall not get leave now until the end of March, but definitely then, I hope.

I hope you are recovered now. Mummy said you had been ill. They certainly ought to promote you or give you less work.

This is the last letter in the collection addressed to Richard's father. He died the following month. The next letter is written after the funeral.

April 18th '43

Dear Mummy

I hope you had a safe journey back to Stoke Mandeville. We had to sit in the corridor all the way down to London. I put Aunt G in a cab to Paddington and shared one part of the way to Charing X with Dorothy McCalmont.

Today my Company Commander and his wife asked me to tea and supper, and we played several sets of tennis. Of course I was dreadful, but no worse than David (my Company Commander).

About that form that I brought you from Holts; don't fill it up until I see you. I understand from Aunt G that there is some complication about a Trust or something and we had best go and see Holt. Aunt G is writing to give me all particulars, and it may affect your pension.

Mummy, you've been so brave and good about it all, I want you to go on in just the same way, because I shall always be worrying about you, and remember I can always come either home or meet you in London if there is *anything* you want to see me about.

April 24th 1943

We have more departures in the Battalion including my Company Commander, and Stevens, so if I don't get my Captaincy I shall go off the deep end properly. But of course the Battalion may be going west. I don't know.


Caterham
May 31st '43

News – definitely news: On Saturday, when we were busily engaged in sending off some more men – whither I do not know, all officers were summoned to BHQ and the Colonel told us that we are being disbanded as a Battalion. He said he would try and get every officer well placed before that happened, and it may well take 2 or 3 months.

It is quite exciting, a sort of end of term feeling. I hope I go somewhere where there is a vacancy for a captain, 'tho as I said before, if one leaves this Battalion it is probable that a pip will come off. However it can't be helped. In the meantime we carry on as if nothing untoward was happening.

We are in the middle of a most boring all day course on Signals – a great waste of time, especially as it is the end of the month, and my busiest time.

We have settled down very comfortably. I've just lost my latest batman but he wasn't very satisfactory. My old batman, Moore, has been wounded in the leg. Apparently they were one of the first Infantry Battalions to enter Tunis.

Sunday 6th June '43

How little new to tell you. The calm before the upheaval, I suppose – but we have been hard at it this week end with an interim Audit board, which has meant much hard work and a loss of valuable time. Yesterday afternoon I attended a local wedding – of the local cinema manager, in the Village Church, and afterwards at the 'Local'. It was quite a good wedding, but no Champagne. However I drank a little Port. Unorthodox at 3 in the afternoon, but better than Gin or Whisky.

The CO has just produced a walking stick like mine. I feel very flattered.

Really there is no news, I like Elliott's book very much. He hits the nail on the head so many times, and with remarkable accuracy. At least to my thinking. No more now.


The Royal Sussex Regiment
10th Battalion
West Hartlepool
Co. Durham
N.B. [July 22 nd 1943]


After many vicissitudes we have arrived and at last a minute in which to write.

As soon as I got back to Caterham, I learnt that the CO is going overseas – and Jerry Jourdain and two other Captains are going this week to my old Mob – but presumably as subalterns. So by now there will really be only a handful left for winding up at Caterham. We had a not too bad journey except that we arrived without our luggage. The idiots who manage the railway at York unhitched our baggage waggon there for some reason known only to themselves, and for a whole night we had nothing at all – not even a toothbrush. However the new lot played up very well and we were lent pyjamas, razors, etc, given a lovely hot bath which we really needed, and a quite comfortable bed.

I find I know here, the CO Colonel Osborne, the 2 in command Major Church, and another Major, Cantrell, and a chap who was in the 6th as a Sergeant, by name Carlton, Bernard Lee who was at Bisley with me, and a fellow called Fleetwood who was very much my junior at Brighton, was next my Batman for 3 days in the 70th at Bexhill, and with whom I am now sharing a room. A very nice chap indeed – but it's a wonderful army is'nt it?

So far my 3rd pip is still on my shoulder. I can only hope!

The weather here is awful, a driving mist all today – bleak and desolate – and ugly – oh the ugliness of it all. Dinner calls, and I must away.


August 12th '43 [West Hartlepool]


Sorry to have been so tardy in writing. Anyway I haven't yet departed from this miserable hole, and there is no evidence as yet that I shall do so immediately. I'm commanding B Company as the Company Commander is away on leave, and we are having quite a strenuous time, on Monday and Tuesday we are going out for a couple of days to do some firing in the Yorkshire Moors – a lonely spot miles from anywhere, but quite pleasant as long as it keeps fine which it rarely does for more than 2 hrs at a stretch.

Yesterday evening I went out to dinner at a little pub with Fleetwood, and we had a real North country sort of high tea, very good and very cheap, with a three quarters of an hour bicycle ride each way. When it got dark we went on Night Ops with the Company and got to bed about two in the morning. I am learning to play golf from Fleetwood, as we have a quite good course here and he is very keen on the game. I haven't made much progress, but hope to improve.

I had a letter from Jerry Jourdain who is with the 6th. He's had to drop a pip, which is rather back luck on him, and he says the officers are changing the whole time so that no one knows anyone else. He also sent remembrances from the few officers who were there when I was – but they are very few.

My batman is going on leave next week, so with a little luck all should turn out well.

The letter you enclosed was from Moore; as far as I can gather they have not moved from Africa.

I shall try and ring up over the week end – only none of the 'phones, there is only one we can use, seem to work properly.

Co Durham
August 19th '43

Dear Mummy

Thank you for yours, and also the Greengages which arrived when we were out on our 2 day exercise; they were much enjoyed by all. We had a good time – a twenty three mile march on the first day – and cooking in the field and sleeping out.

We were right away in the Moors, but there was a funny little pub about 2 miles away to which we repaired in the latish evening, and had a very convivial evening with the locals – who gave us eggs and a large piece of home cured bacon – delicious, but very rich. Next day we spent firing and finally rode home.

When I go I expect to be in convivial company, can't tell you any more than that, but be prepared for anything. You might even see me roll up again one of these fine days, even if only for 48 hrs.

August 29th 1943
[West Hartlepool]

Thank you very much for your letter. I am still here, and likely to be so situate for a week or more. However as an acting Company Commander I've caught a packet of schemes, exercises, and whatnots, quite apart from the normal worries of running a Company. As I told Lalla I was out all last week, and tomorrow I start at an early hour for an unspecified place further North to act as an Umpire in a Division scheme. As soon as I return from that, we have another 3 Day Company scheme on hand: However it is good fun and interesting, and keeps my mind occupied.

I depart in company with 3 officers and some men when we do go, which you will agree is good news, and means I have a better chance of staying with the Regiment. Excuse this writing on different sheets alternately, but I have no blotting paper handy.

I see Paget [1] has a new job, and can guess what it will be! Did you know that they lost their eldest son – is it Julian? – a couple of months ago. I heard the other day from a chap in the Regiment – but I didn't see anything in the papers, and until its confirmed I don't like to write. Do you think you could find out? Please send David's address, and advise him to visit the Golf Club. The steward is Mr Larkham who was a very good friend to me, and will be delighted to see David. He is an old Regular Army Sergeant.

The weather has been fearful for the last week. It really is a dreadful spot. I hear some more of the 70th are coming here shortly.


[West Hartlepool]
Sunday September 12th 1943


Thank you very much for all letters, razor, and hone which have reached me safely. We have had a very busy time and are now on our way somewhere. It was a shame not getting that extra bit of leave, but I was away from Hartlepool on various odd jobs most of the time.

My address until further notice is

The Royal Sussex Regiment

RNBRL

APO 4725

There is no news that I can give now, 'tho I hope to in a few days time. I'm very well, and in high fettle; I know you will keep your spirits up. I hope David manages to get back for his birthday. I have written to him and sent him a present; hope he gets it in time.

# 8

## The Middle East

At last the wait was over, and in mid September 1943
Richard left West Hartlepool for the Middle East. The
first letter describes the voyage out. Frustration continued
for a while, but then he was appointed to help run a Battle
School for the 10<sup>th</sup> Indian Division in Palestine. This took
him into 1944.

October 2<sup>nd</sup> (but probably earlier) 1943
[At Sea]

Well here is the first since we left our native shores –
and we are still at sea, though not for much longer,
I think. It seems a long time since that grey morning
when we slid out of West Hartlepool station, and
several hours later arrived at a port somewhere in
England!

When we arrived there I was relieved to find
that a prisoner for whom I had had to send an
escort, had arrived safely, and I was very surprised
to find that he was a chap who had been in my
Platoon in the 6<sup>th</sup> when we were in France. He
seemed relieved that I was someone he knew, and
has been as good as gold during the voyage. We
went straight on board and the men were settled
in, and we found our own way about.

Quarters are a little cramped but the food has
been excellent all along, and though we made it a
point of honour to eat every course at each meal
for the first few days, I now frequently miss out a
course owing to the warmer weather.

The ship, unfortunately, is dry – you can imagine how appalled I was when the news went round – The thought of gin at 5/- a bottle had been as a guiding light, and from that we had to turn to "soft" drinks: However I can say now that I haven't missed my tipple at all, really, and my predilection for ginger beer, iced, is rapidly assuming the proportions of a passion! We also have a very good shop on board; tobacco is 2/- for a ¼ lb, we are allowed four bars of chocolate a day, soap without coupons, and all sorts of beauty preparations for the ladies, which I am sure have long been unobtainable in England: Also there is a barber, an amazing man who has never been to London in his life – I advised him not to go until after the war.

The first few days the sea was slightly rough but it might have been a raging tempest from the way most stomachs behaved on board. 80% of my men were very sick indeed, and also one of my officers – it was rather dismal. I was quite all right and felt very superior, I don't know why!

We have had an interesting time: The daily routine is reveille 0630, Breakfast 0800 hrs, P.T. 0930 hrs , inspection 10.30 hrs, lunch at midday, tea at a quarter to four, dinner at six, cards for a couple of hours and bed about ten to half past.

In addition there is the usual "Housey Housey", you know, " clickety-click" etc, which I get to watch; I find it too warm to dance. We have quite a good band, one of ours on at all hours, the usual life-boat drill, dances most evenings, these are most amusing.

Today we had the finals of the boxing competition and the Royal Sussex was well to the fore, we won the Middle Weight, and Light-heavy weight contests, and my batman was runner up in the Welter weight final. He would have won I think but his right hand was badly damaged in the semi-finals and the Doctor has told him he must give up boxing for good, which is bad luck. However it was very enjoyable show and the boys were very pleased at the Regiment's success.

For the Officers there are several other duties, I have had to do Field Officer, and subalterns have to do orderly Officer, then there is the business of censoring letters, some business, as these chaps are prolific, if not very accurate, letter writers. Then there is Pay, and rifle inspection, and all the normal little duties.

Washing arrangements are not too bad and I get a salt water bath every evening and after P.T. when I go on that.

I have read a formidable amount of books since I have been on board, including Thomas Hardy's The Mayor of Casterbridge – The last time I read Hardy was on the "City of Mobile" coming back from France in 1940. Rather a coincidence.

I am feeling exceedingly hot at the minute; perspiration absolutely dripping off me. But all the same I am feeling very well, happy, and looking forward with interest to new surroundings.

The weather has been very good all the way. The time I enjoy the most on board this bus is the short period just before blackout when it is just pleasantly cool up on the boat deck, and the sea dead calm, and you get that peculiarly calm and expressionless aspect in the sky, you probably remember many thus on board ship; no wonderful flaming sunset, but the sky from dark blue then green, saffron, and slowly diffusing into pink; anyway, that is the general impression I get, and it is then that my thoughts are especially with you at home, and Daddy, John and David..

Well, this rambling letter must end; I think you have all my news. I can't tell you more for obvious reasons.

October 4th 1943

No 1 Depot Bn  I.T.D  M.E.F.

Hope you have received my letter, airgraph, and telegram by now. I have not yet received anything from you, but I expect it will be not long now. It looks as if I shall be here for some time yet. We are getting acclimatised by doing a little training – so far very gentle – I hope it remains so!

On Saturday the 4 of us visited the local big town. You hitch-hike everywhere and it is about eighteen miles from us. We walked everywhere and had a drink at the French club, and then a very good lunch at the United Services club, and afterwards we bathed, beautifully warm, had tea, and listened to an atrocious band, not nearly so good as the one at our local lido.

Yesterday evening I ran into yet another old school friend, Vivian Edwards, whom I don't suppose you remember – he was in Wilson's with me, and also Johnny Friegard, an ex 70th Battalion Officer; so we hope to see a lot of each other in the near future.

Last night, too, we lost our tent for the first time – a terrific wind and quite a sandstorm – of course it came on just as it was getting dark and we were scuppered for the night – I thought I had lost most of my kit but it has nearly all turned up during the day. It is quite a usual occurrence out here at this time of year. Our lads are getting on all right; we still do a bit of training with them.

We are only allowed to draw the equivalent of £15 per month out here, plus allowances – so

I ought to get a bit of money in the bank soon. These air letters are rationed to one a week – so please give my address to everyone. I shall write to all in time.

October11th1943    [Transit Depot, Middle East]

We are still being acclimatised here – P.T., bathing, weapon training etc. This weekend I went to Cairo. Brigadier Foster who commanded the First Battalion at the time of the Trooping of the Colours in Arundel Park, has just been appointed Colonel of the Regiment  and I was very pleased to get an invitation to a dinner he held at the Turf Club on Saturday evening. We had a very good dinner and I met a lot of old friends and acquaintances. The dinner finished soon after midnight and some of us went along to the Continental Savoy, but could only get iced water at that hour. Most of the jobs in this country seem to be held down by chaps from the Regiment. I heard news of Walter Clarke but he was not present.

On Sunday we saw some of the sights, lunched at Shepherd's Hotel, and went to the Gezira Club in the afternoon. I didn't bathe as I have a slight cold. Cairo is terribly expensive, especially on the little money we are allowed to draw. However I stayed at the Junior Officer's Club – bed and breakfast for 40 piastres which is about 8/- – not bad. Foster was very pleasant and remembered the last occasion on which we met. We had to hitch-hike all the way back – it took us 5 hours!

October 16th 1943 [Transit Depot]

As far as I can gauge, this letter ought to reach you by the 4th November and in it I send all my love and best wishes and Many Happy Returns of the Day, also a very extraordinary photograph of myself taken by the local (Wog) photographer, for the purpose of an Identity Card. It was taken and developed in under ten minutes so I suppose it is not too bad. I do hope that David has been able to get away for your birthday he must be about due for a spot of leave, in any circumstances.

I am quite acclimatised now and have escaped so far the minor ills which most chaps seem to pick up when they arrive: I am now waiting for a posting to one of our Battalions- if I'm lucky- if not, some other Regiment I suppose. I am also on the look-out for any individual jobs that may be going, and intend to see Brigadier Foster if I am here much longer. I have already had an interview for a job and expect to hear something shortly. I shall be away from here for the next fortnight and will be travelling about quite a bit, so I ought to have a pile of letters by the time I arrive.

It is getting cooler here now, 'tho a fortnight ago we experienced the hottest October day for 75 years; it was the night we lost our tent, which I told you about.

You remember the nation that took "Halton"?[1] We had their "Top Dog" on board our ship. That was why I was so pleased when we won the Royal Guard Mounting competition.

The food here is not too good: Very little variety, and badly cooked; however I do pretty well, and always have an appetite. The Bar is adequate, and we get a bar and cigarette ration once a week. Tomorrow evening I am dining with John Friegard at his Mess. He used to be in the 70th with me a very nice fellow.

In the evenings I manage to get a game of cards, or chess, or draughts, and of course I am doing quite a bit of reading. We also know now where the English flies go in the winter time: I have bought a fly whisk from a persistent vendor in Ismalia, but it aint much use. No more now; A very happy birthday and love to all.

Trafalgar Day 1943  [2]
[Palestine]

In case my other letter doesn't reach you in time Many Happy Returns of the 4th and all my love and best wishes – I am writing this in Nazareth, North Palestine where I shall be for a few days. We are encamped on a hill side East of the village which is on the other side of the valley, and it was a beautiful sight this morning when the sun rose suddenly and lighted on the white village opposite. It really is a pretty place high up in the hills, and the air is delightfully fresh – though the nights are chilly – after Egypt.

We took 2and½ days travelling here by car. The first stage of the journey was up to Ismalia, where we crossed the canal, then right across the Sinai desert, very hot, and a very bumpy ride, then we crossed the border into Palestine, passed through Beersheba and Gaza, to a transit camp near Jaffa where we spent the night. Next day we had to go to Jaffa and Tel Aviv which is a wholly Jewish town and seemed very pleasant with a grand situation on the Mediterranean.

Then in the afternoon we began our journey again, pushed on to Jerusalem where we stayed the night. We didn't get a chance to see the sights, but hope to when we go back. Yesterday morning we left Jerusalem, passed through the hills – it's an incredibly hilly country – stopped at Jacob's well, where Christ drank the water, near Nablus, crossed the Plain of Esdrailon and so up into the hills to Nazareth. Can't get any more into this letter but will write again soon.

October 23rd 1943
[Palestine]

I hope you got your two birthday letters on time. I am still in Palestine and we are seeing all the countryside, except up to now we haven't penetrated the Jordan valley or Jericho – I hear that Jericho is a miserable hole anyway. I am working with a Polish Brigade for the next few days, and it is most interesting – I have my own interpreter, and we have great fun trying to get things straight. Their food is rather amazing. We have a very small breakfast, an enormous lunch, and tea just runs into supper. There are three other English Officers with me – three Majors – and as a concession to our queer ways we are allowed milk with our tea. Anyway, I am thoroughly enjoying it.

Last night was our first sleeping in the open, and sure enough last night the rainy season opened with five showers during the night; it has also rained intermittently, but quite heavily, today – At sun rise this morning the East was one enormous red glow with a dark curtain of rain sweeping down between us and the hills round Jerusalem.

All the country round here is studded with olive groves and orange groves. They are picking the olives now – I think they are of the olive oil variety – too small for eating and the oranges will be ready before the end of November. Last year there was a glut of them and you could buy a camel load for a piastre about 2and ½ pence. Would you like a sheepskin coat for birthday and Christmas combined? They look beautiful.

November 3rd 1943
[Written from Transit Depot]

A terrific wind has just sprung up and I doubt not that our tent will be down in a very few minutes. Here is an account of my wanderings through Palestine. By now you will have received my earlier air letters with news of our wanderings up to Oct 23rd.

We stayed down near Ramlek until the 25th and as I was at Polish Brigade H.Q. we had a very good time. They were all eager to speak English and in addition I had my interpreter recently arrived from Russia, where he had spent some time as a guest!! Of the USSR. On the Monday we began moving up North again until we were North West of Lake Tiberius, the Sea of Galilee. The exercise ended on Friday morning, after two sleepless nights and an attack over 8 miles of the roughest going imaginable. The spirit of the troops was magnificent – all they live for is to get their teeth into the huns. On Friday I stayed the night there – Next morning we set off for Jerusalem, lunched at the Police HQ. It was too late to do any sightseeing that night so we dined at a café and went to a cinema – the first since leaving England.

Next morning I set off by myself, as the others wanted to be lazy, to see the old city. First of all I went to High Mass at the Latin Patriarchate. It was a magnificent service with wonderful singing, and all the ceremony that I love. The organ played Handel and Brahms, and the sermon was preached by a Franciscan Monk. As it happened it was a

Feast Day, reinstituted after many hundreds of years by the late Pope, the feast of Christ the King.

From there, I went to the Church of the Holy Sepulchre which is built over Calvary. It is a fine building – originally set up by the Mother of the Emperor Constantine in the 4th Century AD. It is served by 5 churches, the Catholic, Greek Orthodox, Coptic, Syrian and Armenian, each of which has its chapel. A barbarically beautiful building, dark, incense filled, and very inspiring. It contains the Tomb of Christ, the place where the cross stood, the place where Joseph of Arimathea washed the body of Christ and took it to the sepulchre.

After that I walked round the old city, and visited the actual 14 stations of the Cross, and the prison where Christ and Barabbas lay and the place where Pilate gave judgement. Finally I visited the wailing wall where the wailing was of a pretty high standard.

In the afternoon we all went down to Jericho and the Dead Sea, a drop of over 3000 feet from Jerusalem. The Dead Sea is about 900 feet below sea level. It is an uneasy spot to stay in, very hot and arid, and we were quite glad to return to the hills.

At 5 o'clock Sunday evening I went to the service in the Church of the Holy Sepulchre for the Procession round the fourteen stations of the Cross. It is carried out every night by the Catholic and Greek Orthodox. I joined the Catholic Procession. Wonderful unaccompanied singing, the Priests, followed by the Monks and the Nuns, and a whole number of Pilgrims. Everyone carried a lighted candle. It was an unbelievably impressive sight and I have never heard such beautiful chanting. I am terribly glad I went – it made it all seem so real.

Next morning we visited Bethlehem – where we saw the stable and the manger, over which the church of the Nativity is built. I bought the Christmas cards there and a little broach for you and Lalla for Christmas which I hope you will like.

I enclose my Certificate of Pilgrimage which is quite interesting. The old boy doesn't normally fill in the name himself so I felt quite honoured.

10th Indian Div H.Q.

M.E.F. [Palestine]

12th November 1943

I am sorry that there has been a bit of a gap between my last and this, but as you see I have moved my tent and pitched it up in the Galilean mountains, along with the 10th Indian Div.

Briefly the story is in this wise: I was asked if I would like to go and start a battle school in 10th Div. As there was no immediate chance of reaching the 1st Battalion I said I would. So I was sent off to Cairo for an interview, which was apparently satisfactory, and together with another chap – Indian Army, name Mitchell, a nice fellow – we were told to catch the next train to Palestine – In passing we were both – having been accepted – told to take down our 3rd pip, there was no place on the establishment. Comment superfluous, they are being very decent in the Div, and we are hoping to get that pip back again very soon, but when they asked for instructors they said specifically Majors or Captains, but apparently temporary Captains didn't count with G.H.Q.

Anyway it is good to be doing something, and the climate here is very nice, but exceedingly cold once the sun has gone down. We are in a very pleasant Mess, much better food than the I.T.D., and we are just returned from a recce of the proposed site of the school – I shall probably be here about three months.

November 14th 1943

[Palestine. 10th Indian Div]

Yesterday we went down to Tiberias on the Sea of Galilee, and had lunch at the local pub. Who did I meet there but Walter, of all people, in all places. He is with the 4th Battalion many miles away and was just over for a spot of duck shooting on Lake Hula. He is getting married in 3 months time and I shall be his Best Man D.V.! I was very pleased to see him, just the same but a lot older and he's been knocked about quite a bit, and won't go into battle again as he's not fit.

Its very lovely down on the Sea of Galilee, and we went to where Jordan leaves the lake, a very narrow, deep-flowing and swift river. You might ask the local Parson if he would like some Jordan water – and I'll bring him some back. Our camp is nearly 3000 feet above sea level, and the Sea of Galilee is 680 feet below sea level. We look straight down from our eyrie on to the lake and often there is a sea of cloud in between. Beyond the sea and slightly to the right we can see Mount Tabor where the Prophetess Deborah lived, behind us to the right is the tallest mountain in Palestine Jemmul Jarmaq, and 35 miles behind us on the left is Mount Hermon, 7000 feet, so we are in very picturesque surroundings.

It will be some time before our school gets going. We are just doing the spade work at the minute. I played Bridge the other evening – first time here and had a disastrous evening, losing 50 piastres – about 10/-, not a card all the evening, but I hope for better luck next time.

Our French friends are causing a spot of bother up the road [3]- what is the opinion in England?

November 22nd 1943
[Palestine]

Sorry this letter is a trifle overdue, but we are all on our own at the present, and I couldn't get hold of my weekly ration. We are still in the same place but the Div has moved for the time being, and four of us have a very cosy little Mess, and feed much better than we have for a long time.

The Major who is going to command the whole battle school arrived last week, and on Friday he and I went down South to make another recce. We had to call in at Jerusalem to see someone in authority, and we lunched at the King David Hotel. Towards the end of the meal a Padre came in whom I thought I recognised. I walked towards him and on closer inspection saw I was mistaken. As I turned away a hand gripped my arm, and someone said "Hello Richard", and there in solitary state and warm English clothes was Dr. Keane – you could've knocked me down "wiv a fevver". He had come by plane from Cairo, and is on a mission inspecting and appraising the agricultural possibilities of all countries in the Middle East with a view to coordination of supplies – or something like that. Tony is still in North Africa, and Bevin at home. Was it not an extraordinary meeting – he was so far from my mind that for a minute I couldn't place him at all.

We returned via Jerusalem from Gaza next day, and I lunched with him and chatted about old times.

It is exceedingly cold up here now; not bad in the day, but icy at night. I expect to see snow on Mount Hermon any day now. By the way, it's 10,000 feet, not 7000 as I think I said last time-Well, I must stop now, hope everyone is well and spirits high.

November 26ᵗʰ 1943

[Lebanon]

You will be pleased to hear that my Captaincy has been restored, from the date when it was taken down. The mistake, as I knew it was, was made back at Cairo – anyway everything is now as it was. We have come down from our mountain retreat and are now in the Lebanon, very interesting, but I don't think we will stay here long, as the old Battle School is at last getting cracking, and we hope to open the first course by the middle of December. There is an awful lot to be done, training the demonstration Platoon, getting stores, preparing schemes, choosing locations and a hundred more little things.

Thank you also for Blackwoods, it will be a great boon when it arrives – Easily the best reading magazine.

The money situation in this country is fantastic; I had lunch in Beirut yesterday and the bill was about £3 which was equal to about 4/-. Of course it's the French pound, and not worth very much, according to our ideas of the pound.

It is much warmer here than in the mountains, and I may go bathing this afternoon. I had a long talk last night with a chap in the Sappers who met

Shoosmith – you remember him at the RMC – and he is a cousin of Glenorchy's, so we covered a lot of ground, and drank some excellent Cyprus brandy. Well, I must stop now. Hope everyone is well.

December 3rd 1943
[Palestine]


As you see we are in our new location, and up to our eyes in work as we open on the 18th December. I am rushing about preparing exercises, building assault courses, training demonstration Platoons, etc. As a result, none of us have had any time to do anything, 'tho last night three of the chaps went to Tel Aviv for the evening – I was on duty and stayed behind – Also I was not feeling quite up to a "night out". I received yours of the 15th this evening. Glad you are getting the letters through O.K. and congratulations to David on getting substance of a subalterns rank. It often takes a long time for authority to wear it, to come through.

Our new camp is very pleasant, well appointed wooden Officers and Sergeants Messes, Mens Canteens, Offices etc. I have secured a bedroom in one of the huts with electric light. In fact all the permanent staff are similarly accommodated. I have just heard that Shoosmith is in the Div, though I haven't met him yet. I think I told you this in my last letter. I am looking forward to seeing him.

We had a game of vingt-et-un in the Mess t'other night, I won a small sum – But I miss my bridge – we were playing most evenings up at Div HQ – I was quite sorry, in a way, to leave that Mess, we had some very nice fellows in it. The Arabs in this area are a damned nuisance – always pinching stuff. But they give oranges away free.

December 12th 1943
[Palestine]

The weekly letter, a bit late again I'm afraid. We are now not opening until after Christmas, but lots of work to do all the same. In fact, the amount of "laying on" is really formidable, and we are grateful for the weeks reprieve – We are going to spend Christmas here, usual dinner and men's dinner, but are hoping to go to the midnight Mass at Bethlehem, and then spend a few hours at Jerusalem; Probably the only chance I shall get, as I don't suppose we shall be anywhere near Palestine next year. We might with luck even be home.

Thankyou for the Bible and Blackwoods. I expect they will be here soon after Christmas. I had a letter from David t'other day – he seems to be spending his whole time on schemes.

Last night we were invited to the Palestine Police Mess after dinner. When we got there we found they were already very merry, and we had a convivial evening. I regret to say I remained sober the whole time, and felt very fit this morning, but two of the party stayed in bed until lunch time. Unfortunately they got on to Arack, which is a villainous poison. I couldn't stand the smell of it.

The other day on a reconnaissance I stumbled on the remains of the city of Lachish, an ancient Philistine city, very interesting perched on a mound about 300 feet high in a flat plain. In fact travelling about fitting up schemes, I'm frequently finding interesting facts, sites, and fitting my history to the ground.

December18<sup>th</sup> 1943
[Battle School, Palestine]

Thank you for four letters this week. Your remarks about the "dry" cold in Palestine are rather ironic now, as the rains began two days ago – out of a blue sky and a warm West wind came rain, and it is now decidedly chilly.

We now find that many of our schemes will have to be modified as the rain makes a lot of places quite ungetatable, or impassible to transport – however we will survive it, 'tho continual rain will make our outdoor programme a very wet affair – thank goodness for the hot showers! We are extremely busy here before the course opens, especially with Christmas coming in between.

I have just invested in a beautiful pair of rubber gum boots – for 10/- at the Officer's shop. They are going to be worth their weight in gold this winter – the mud, even after 20 minutes rain is terrible.

Thank you for transcribing Watts letter – it makes me rather embarrassed, Heaven knows why he got such a good opinion of me – I cursed him often enough. Still it is pleasant to hear from these chaps. I have written to him; I hope he gets your/ my airgraph in time for Christmas.

Damn all Lawyers, Bankers, and the Y--- S--- Government; <sup>4</sup>cheats, rogues, liars, perculators, usurers and everything else. Don't let them worry you too much – hope this arrives in time to bring a Better New Year to you and all at home.

Boxing Day 1943
[Battle School, Palestine]

Christmas over, and we are now getting down to brass tacks. The students are arrived, or most of them, and we begin at crack of dawn tomorrow with an opening lecture by the Div Commander.

I hope it all goes off successfully. We knocked off work on Friday morning and I set off to Jerusalem with two of our Officers, in my jeep. Luckily there was some official business to be transacted, or it might have been frowned on if only for pleasure. We went to the King David and had a drink, but I was disappointed not to meet someone I knew, Dr Keane having left for Cyprus. We lunched at the Officer's Club, and then went out to Bethlehem to reconnoitre the evening service. We couldn't get any tickets for the midnight service or the service in the actual grotto but we decided to attend the carol singing in the courtyard of the church.

We went back to Jerusalem and met a lot of chaps from Div HQ, had an early dinner and hit the road again. I've never seen such crowds on the road – it was worse than a weekend trek to Brighton, or Derby Day – However we arrived in time, and avoided the army car park, and visited the stable where Christ was born. It was very impressively decorated and even more so was the enormous crowd moving round the church above in almost complete darkness. The carols were quite good – did you hear them on the radio?

We had a very cold drive back. We left the Officer's Club at midnight and the journey took us nearly an hour and a half. On Christmas day we first of all entertained the Sergeants in the Officer's

Mess. Then we served the men's dinner and made speeches and all that sort of thing; at tea time I went over and saw Shoosmith and talked over old times. He's married to a Greek woman, she's in Cyprus. Then in the evening we had our Christmas dinner and wound up with a protracted visit to the Sergeant's Mess. Not a bad Christmas, I'm afraid I shall suffer for it when we begin taking violent exercise.

# 9

## Battling on in Palestine

A new year has begun, and Richard is still with the Battle School in Palestine. Elsewhere in the world, British and American forces were fighting in Italy, and on the Eastern front the Russians had recaptured much of their territory. War was also being fiercely fought against Japan in the Far East.

10 Indian Div Battle School M.E.F.
[Palestine]

January 2nd 1944

The first week of our first course has sped by. We began on Monday, and I'm afraid that I had to send back five Officers so far, as being quite unfit, for various reasons, to go on with the course. I had no idea that they would find it so strenuous. But it's good fun and the time literally flies – up at six o'clock in the morning and I hope to be finished for the day by 7 in the evening.

Coming back this afternoon from a jaunt to the Field cashier – who wasn't in – I saw a Royal Sussex cap badge standing by the side of the road. It turned out to be Jimmy James, who left the 70th with Kimber and Prescott, and it now in the 45th with Walter Clarke. He is down here on a course, so I hope to see quite a bit of him in the next three weeks. Walter's girl has just broken off the engagement, he tells me, and Walter himself is in a spot of trouble over some arms that were pinched by some Wogs – so I shan't be his best man after all.


January 9th 1944
[Battle School, Palestine]


We have finished the second week of the course and I am glad to say that no one else has dropped out, they all seem to be thoroughly enjoying it. The General visited us on Thursday, staying to lunch, and seemed very pleased with all that he saw. He even went through the "Battle Innoculation" course. We've only got one more week now, the most interesting I think, and also the toughest.

On Friday evening I went to the Punjab Regiment's Twelfth Night party – at Shoosmith's invitation and a very good show it was too. About 80 Officers were there, and I met a fellow called Mullins who was in a squad which I used to take in weapon training at Chichester in the early days of the war. He was commissioned into the Cheshires, and from them went to the Punjab Regiment.


I think when the three months of this course are over I shall try and get into one of the units of this Div, if they will have me. I see no hope of going to the Regiment and I don't want to go near the I.T.D. if I can help it.

The weather is frightful at present – exceedingly cold, a foul wind, and torrents of rain – in fact early this morning we had hail, I should think there might be snow up in the hills round Jerusalem.

January 15th
[Battle School, Palestine]

Well, here I be, quite exhausted at the end of the first course which I think has gone tolerably well. I have been very fortunate in my section instructors and demonstration Platoon – they have all worked exceedingly hard. The students seem to have enjoyed the course, and I have learned a great deal myself. Unfortunately on our big scheme it rained torrents all day, and susceptible as ever I caught a rotten cold which prevented me going out last night to celebrate the end of the course. Instead I went to bed with a hot drink and a couple of aspirins and feel a lot better today. We begin our next course in a weeks time, so I shall be thoroughly rested and refreshed by then. Of course, there is a lot of revision and practising to be done.

On Tuesday we were visited by the Brigadier Infantry, the big pot at Cairo who is in charge of training. We put on a demonstration for him, which everyone since has said was the best we did. Who do you think he turned out to be? Brigadier James VC DSO MC, my old CO in the second Battalion. I was terribly pleased to see him, and he appeared pleased to see me. We had a long talk and then saw the demonstration which I think pleased him. Extraordinary the people I seem to be bumping in to. I have also had a letter from Tony Ball who used to be the MO in the 6th Battalion; I think he is now in Italy. I met him in Cairo when I was up there on an interview in November.

I have also managed to contact Moore – who, alas, has got a batman's job up in Syria. He is attached to a similar sort of school as this. He has been downgraded owing to his eyesight, I don't suppose he will see any more fighting this war.

The weather has really been wicked this last week. Very cold with howling gusts of rain. It gets right into your bones. For the first time for weeks I have got the wireless to myself and am enjoying a pleasant Sunday afternoon's concert. Quite like Sunday afternoons at home.

January 30th 1944
[Battle School, Palestine]

Just finished a very busy week – the first week of our second course. It opened in very sad circumstances with the death of our Div Commandar – General Lloyd, which I expect you saw in the papers. He was killed in a car accident while umpiring a scheme down in Egypt. Everyone in the Div is very upset, as he was very popular and a good Commander. And of course we owe our existence as a school to him and he always took great interest in it. Now the great question is who will succeed him. We should know soon I suppose.

We had lovely weather all last week, warm and windless, which lasted precisely until midday yesterday, when we pack up for a little recreation. Since then we've been suffering the worst weather I've experienced out here – thunder, lightening, hail, and continual very heavy showers. Our electric light has packed in – let's hope its all right before nightfall.

Coming back from Jerusalem last night we twice passed vehicles off the road, sunk deep in mud. We could do nothing for them except ring up the recovery section when we got back.

Thank you very much for the Bible which has arrived absolutely unharmed. I am very glad to have it – there is always something I want to refer to in it.

February 5th 1944

Thank you very much for yours of 20th January.
I'm glad to say they seem to be coming through fine
now. Also this week I received my first Blackwoods
magazine; and a grand number it is too. Did you
see the ballad by Bernard Fergusson at the end of it.
Do you remember him, an instructor at Sandhurst?
I also received 2 unidentified books, which must
have come from Aunt G but there was no letter or
note. A book from Kitty also arrived so you see
I am, very gratefully, snowed under by a spate of
literature of all types. I told you in my last letter,
did I not, that Aunt K's book had arrived.

I have had some very unexpected letters this
week. One from an old 70th Battalion RSM Ward
who is now at ITC Colchester and grumbling like
anything but I think secretly enjoying himself. He
addressed me in his letter as "Dear Sir Richard",
do you consider this a portent? Another letter was
from Martin Prescott with the 2nd giving me lots of
news of old friends and himself, and yet another
was from Gibbin, who was one of my Corporals
in France, and with whom, until recently, I have
corresponded regularly. Very good to hear again.

We've had a perfect week this week, the rain
stopped on Sunday night and we have enjoyed six
days of almost English Summer weather at its best.
Tonight I am going to dinner at the local Officers
Club at Gaza with the CO, and several Officers of
the Manchesters.

February 14<sup>th</sup> 1944
[Battle School, Palestine]

Thank you for two letters this week, one dated Jan 26<sup>th</sup>, the other Feb 1<sup>st</sup>. Also I was very pleased to receive the Jan issue of Blackwoods, it arrived a week after the December one. The mail seems to be coming along fine now. You should certainly have received my small parcel containing two broaches, mother of pearl, from Bethlehem.

We've finished our second course now and I think it was a great improvement on the first and we hope to make the third even better. I've had a grand week this last week, as I met two old friends who are doing a course near here, Martin Prescott and Peter Chettle. Of course you remember Martin, but Peter I haven't seen for four years – he was at Brighton with me and one of my greatest friends. .....I decided to take him in hand, and all this week -end I've been making him go out and meet people, we went to Jerusalem yesterday and I acted as guide. I think he has improved 100% in the last two days – quite his old cheerful self. I am dining with him and Martin on Wednesday and they are coming over to our Mess on Friday.

February 18<sup>th</sup> 1944
[Battle School, Palestine]

Now we are nearly at the end of our week off – saddled with a new course starting on Monday. In addition we have now an extra wing here – so terrific chaos will ensue no doubt, as they are one of our gallant allies, and naturally have no language in common.

126

Tonight Martin and Peter are coming to dinner with me. Martin has made a great impression on my brother Officers here, he has a store of songs some clever, some vulgar, but all amusing. I'm not so sure about Peter, he's inclined to pack in when there's anyone else about.... It's being attached to the "Rice Corps" (Indian Army Service Corps) that is festering his soul  He won't even wear his African Campaign ribbon, says he has done nothing to deserve it. Silly ass!

There doesn't seem to be much news, we've just had the first Khamseen (or however you spell it) of the season, a terrible blistering hot wind that makes you feel dreadful, and creates sand storms. I went to bed the afternoon it began – very pleasant too – but you can't stay in bed for a day and a half – its blowing a gale even now – most unpleasant.

I never write during courses except home, so I have thousands to answer in the break – Just finished one to Moore. He told me to write to you more frequently!

February 27th 1944

The tea you gave Andy made my teeth go gnash together and my mouth to water. My ideal tea, I love eggs boiled at tea time. As a matter of fact the other day my room-mate George Keogh managed to buy some eggs and we had a couple each for tea – wish they had been home brewed! Thank you also for the delicious shaving soap which arrived in fine condition the other day. The day before it arrived I had bought some horrible Palestinian muck and thrown it away it stank! Now I look forward to shaving every morning – gets me up early – sounds like an advert for some well known brand – but I was glad to see the name "Penhaligan" on it. Thank you very much.

Young Peter Chettle stayed at the school until Wednesday, as he suddenly got a signal saying his crowd were on the move and would pick him up. We had a good time in Jerusalem on Saturday and Sunday, and I met a whole crowd of chaps I know or whose brothers I know. We had a very merry party. Chettle returned to the school with me and we had several games of bridge when the third course began (last Monday), and of course talked and talked and talked.

We have just got a new Div Commander – General Reid, who escaped from a POW camp in Italy. He sounds a good fellow.

It is terribly warm today the good weather seems to be returning apace. Hope it doesn't get too hot while the school is running.


March 5th 1944
[Battle School, Palestine


A lovely evening, with the scented smell of wood burning in the air – and we are about to begin the last week of the third course.

Really very little news; it has been so hot here that on Friday I went into Khaki Drill and felt much better, and so, of course, it absolutely pelted down on Saturday. Today, however, warm and beautiful – the countryside is completely green – with crops – the Arab really is very industrious for two months of the year, everything ploughed up, including our training areas. For the rest of the year he toils not at all, but lives on his crops, except of course during the fig, grape and olive seasons – But heaven knows when they arrive. The oranges and grapefruit are just about over now, and the lemons will be in two or three weeks. I do wish I could have sent you some, but they wouldn't stand the voyage. – I've taken to having a pure lemon juice at lunch time, occasionally, very good indeed after a hard open air morning! Nearly as good as beer.

I hope you are feeling really tip top now – the winter must be nearly over – do you remember the beautiful March weather last year – All my thoughts with you on the 17th of this month.[1]

# 10

## Special Operations Executive

SOE – Special Operations Executive – was formed in 1940. Richard learnt about the possibility of joining SOE while he was in the Middle East. Against the wishes of Colonel Foster, who thought he should go to Staff College, he managed to join the organisation. SOE was founded to liaise with anti-fascist groups in enemy territory, to cause disruption behind enemy lines, and to keep enemy forces occupied away from the major centres of war. His training took place in Palestine, a country he had begun to love while he was with the Battle School. The letters which follow reveal a new strength and a romantic view of the lands of Palestine, Lebanon and Syria.

Royal Sussex Regiment
c/o no 1 Bn  ITD  MEF
[Cairo]

March 18<sup>th</sup> 1944

So much has happened, and in such a short space of time that I really don't know where to begin. In the first place, don't write to me at the above address as I'm not there now, and hope that I shan't go there at all.

Last Saturday we arrived back from Jerusalem having celebrated the ending of our third course! We found that we had twelve hours to pack the whole place up. Well of course no one had any

time for me. They gave me a movement order –
thanked me very much for what I had done, and
said that a nice letter would go through about my
work. Sorry everything had finished so suddenly!

Well, I saw that once again the work of months
was going to bring no reward, so I popped off to
Cairo – where I am now, and saw Uncle B, [1] and in
a few days I hope to be able to wire you my new
address.

I can't tell you anything about the job I hope to
get, but it will be very interesting and useful. If I
pull it off. The result of the interview will be known
on Tuesday or Wednesday, so you may receive a
wire before you get this letter. Uncle B is very fit
and sends his love.

What a difference it makes beginning on the
office boys from the top, instead of the bottom – I
feel if I pull this off, it will be through no merit
of my own, but my fortunate relationship with
Uncle B.

No more now – don't worry about the third
pip – they juggle me about as if I were an inanimate
object. With love to all from Richard

March 26th 1944
[Transit Depot]

I hoped to be able to give you a few more details
by the time I came to write this letter – but alas
– as yet my posting has not come through 'tho I
feel it cannot be more than a matter of 48 hours
now – However I am still without an address, but
if you like, write to me as above, and I may get it
– I will let you know my new address as soon as I
know it myself.

I am beginning to be a bit bored living this lotus eating life at a transit camp. I have read on an average a book a day for the last week, and apart from a few odd duties, and a local dance, have done nothing else. Each day I have put off writing to you as I felt news is bound to come *today*, but no luck. I haven't seen Uncle B again – don't wish to disturb him too much, he's terribly busy.

The last two days have been very muggy, with the horrible hot desert wind blowing – most unpleasant, but luckily two baths a day is the order here – which is pleasant.

I quite miss my violent exercise, having been used to it for the last three months, and keep wanting to go out and throw a bomb at something or someone. Two things I've gained in the last few months a knowledge of explosives, and an appalling blood thirstyness, not like my usual self I'm afraid.

The Royal Sussex Regiment
HQ Force 133   MEF
March 28th 1944

Just a line to drop you my latest address – So you will realise that I've got the job I wanted. It came through the day after I wrote to you – most annoying, but I hope this will catch you before you've written to me c/o the ITD.

I can't tell you anything about my new job, except that it is very interesting, and I am very keen on it. I shall shortly be returning to the country where we had our Battle School.

No news, I'm afraid, but very pleased. I don't expect I shall get a letter from you for my birthday, but that will be due to lack of address. If you are still using the old address it is just possible I may get the letters eventually.

April 6th 1944
[Palestine – SOE]

Very belatedly, I'm afraid, but all my love and thoughts for you all at home, for Easter, and the first anniversary of April 12th. [2] I've had a slight cold during the last few days and have been in bed for the last two; however I now feel completely recovered – luckily the course does not begin until Sunday so I missed nothing very much – While waiting for everyone to arrive we have been doing a little light work, but very interesting. This course lasts about five weeks, and we will be working fairly hard – seven days a week. We are pleasantly situated here, plenty of fresh air, and a few cafes within easy reach for an evening's mild dissipation.

Since the Battle School broke up I have had no letters from you – but I was not very hopeful as the Indian Div Postal Authorities have remarkably little idea of efficient organisation, and no damn brain at all – they work on a series of pre conceived, and, needless to say, utterly erroneous ideas – So I don't suppose I will ever get my February "Blackwoods", or your March letters.

Prospects of a Bridge four this evening – and if that fails I may get a game of chess – and if that ain't forthcoming I may throw dice in the Bar – which is excellent – with an old Brightonian who is on the course – 'tho he was at Brighton several years before me. Still it is very pleasant to meet everyone. The other day I met Johnny Fleetwood, just before I left Cairo, and several old Royal Sussex men – Grand fellows.

April16th 1944
[Palestine, SOE]

Here's a birthday letter, I expect you have written to me, but as yet I have had not a single letter for the last month. Of course they will take a few days longer now, as they go to HQ first, and then come up here where we are doing our course.

We have just completed the first week of the course, very interesting, and very hard work, not so much physically, as lectures etc. We begin at 7:30 in the morning and finish at 7 o'clock in the evening, with one hour off for lunch, and one for tea – so it is quite a long day – we also work Sundays, and next weekend we are out on a scheme. We have just put the clocks on, about ten days ago, and the longer evenings are very pleasant. For the first time this year we had a wonderful view of Mount Hermon, snow capped, standing right out above the small hills. So the weather is beginning to clear up, though it rained today.

We have a wonderful conglomeration of nationalities on the course, including a Yank, a Czeck, a Greek, and a chap from Rhodesia, a mixed bag, but we all get on very well together. I have had three "bridge" nights in the last week and won every rubber, with a good partner and luck; we don't play very late usually as we are rather tired. How little news there is; I hope my third pip may return to me one day. It must be very pleasant in the country now, I suppose the cuckoo is arrived, and the trees just burgeoning.

Have you now shaken off all your winter ills – a few remains of my cold are still in evidence, but are being gradually banished by the healthful properties of a cold shower nearly every morning.

April 29th 1944
[Palestine SOE]

Sorry to be so late with this letter. We were out on a scheme last week, over the weekend, and quite honestly not one minute have I had, until today to write. We have the whole day off, a half term holiday, and tomorrow we begin another scheme lasting several days. I am glad to say in the last four days I have received your letters dated March 2nd, 16th, and April 4th, 9th, and 16th; so I've quite caught up with the news. They sent some on from ITD, so perhaps I will get the shaving soap after all. Thank you very much for it.

I have lost severely by instructing at the Battle School, as I have now had an airgraph from Cox and Kings saying that my return to subaltern's rank is backdated to the day I joined the staff of the school i.e. in November. That means they will dock my pay for the next few months. It is most irritating and I do feel that I have been imposed upon by the GI of 10 Div, the training team, and the whole God damned lot of them. I am very glad to be where I am now – far more congenial.

Rather a grumbling letter I'm afraid – But nowadays it appears to be part of a British Officer's Training in no case to keep his word.


May 6th 1944
[Palestine SOE]

Thank you for yours of April 24th which arrived today lunchtime. The address you have as above is my permanent address, all letters you send me come through HQ Force 133, and mine to you go there to be censored. That, I think, accounts for the slightly longer time that our letters take.

We had an arduous exercise over the weekend – but good fun, 'tho I felt flat out at times. One morning we had a marvellous breakfast, having lived on the rations we carried for some days, a real Jorrocksian breakfast – missing only the good old English ale, we had three eggs apiece, fried chicken, liver, fried potatoes, peas, beans, carrots and cabbage, followed by a whole roast pigeon, chips, vegetables etc, bread and coffee galore – nearly put me off my marching stroke the next day! This course has only a week to run now, and then we go on another one for a week or so. Very interesting.

We have begun bathing, still a bit cold 'tho. Best love to Lalla, and of course Punch, and Judith.[3]

May 16th 1944
[Lebanon SOE]

At last arrived at my new course. This letter is rather, I'm afraid, overdue. We finished at Haifa on Saturday and we were packed off straightway to the Lebanon – as this course only assembles tomorrow we have had three days leave – in beautiful Syria, delightful, civilized, French influenced Lebanon – and yet they want to get rid of the French – technically, I suppose, already they have. Yet this land is French, emotively and actually – the towns look like France – and it's so nice to hear the people speaking French – to see the cavalry clatter through the streets; in what other army would they smoke their cigarettes "en route".

I decided to go to Damascus – Peter Chettle was stationed nearby 'tho I knew not exactly where. We left Beirut – a kind Colonel gave me a lift the first 50 kilometres – down miles of lilac lined avenue then straight up the hills – pretty villages with hotels preparing for the summer season and then suddenly we were above the snow line and the snow still lying in the crevices. We gained the top of the pass and saw the long narrow valley in which lies Baalbeck, Heliopolis of old, and beyond, the range that separated me from Damascus.

With surprise Hermon came on to view to the South East – it changes shape so easily and gracefully. I love Mount Hermon – wherever I am I look for him.. And so we parted, my Colonel to Baalbeck and I to sit by the roadside appealing for a lift which came twenty minutes later in the shape of a monstrous big American Staff car, piloted, there is no other word for it, by a large American – and as we sped across the fertile valley land huge tank Transporters appeared and my heart sank for I knew they were Peter's and where was he going.

And then I saw him standing Peteresquely by his truck so my astonished car stopped, and I descended, walking down the road I was espied from afar and greeted heartily – He, alas, was out for three days – if my letter had ever reached he need not have gone – but [he advised] "go to my camp which lies but five leagues from the city of Saul's blindness, and there you will meet George Dickie-Clarke". How the Clarks occur in my life – and he will receive you and entertain you. So stopping another American car I went on my way. More of this saga tomorrow. I must stop now. Our course begins.

May 19th 1944 – Canto the Third
[Lebanon SOE]

And so progressing, at one o'clock I met my red-haired host – Dickie Clark – a very nice chap – S. African, and was at Cambridge when I was at the RMC – went to India with Peter and been with him ever since. Never have I met anyone I liked more at first sight. We lunched at a French restaurant – I ate frogs legs – very succulent and fat – have you ever – they were delicious. We drank a local wine – quite good. Talked we so much that it was half past three before we left to see the old city and haunt the familiar places of Doughty and Burton and Wilfred Blunt – and the long forgotten palaces and courts of Saladin – the destroyer of the 3rd Crusade, the image of Paynim chivalry – Lord of Islam and possessor of Egypt, Palestine and Syria.

His palace – El Azam – lies in the populous part – But in its courts no sound but the birds song and the fountains falling. I can't describe the rooms, but we could have sat in one of them all day. The orange trees, the water, the carp, the rich colours and the peace of a world past.

And so we went to the great Mosque, where Greeks built, where Roman temple stood – where Roman pillars still stand. Five hundred prayer mats given of Mecca, of Sultan Ma'hmoud, of Sultan Abdel Hamid. And the tomb of the great Saladin with its green turban, and relic of Kaiser William Hohenzollern.

Then weary, we went to shop, we drank their coffee and I have for you what I think is the most beautiful brocade in the world – genuine 17th century pattern – of course the stuff itself is modern, but six men cannot tear it. I could only afford a yard but it is 54 inches wide and will make a beautiful little jacket or whatever you will – it cost Pounds Syrian Fifty Two – not really expensive – nearly £7 a yard but you could probably get at least £10 for it – it is a spiritual investment – a design for living, in cloth. I hope it will arrive soon. No more room now but will continue the saga tomorrow. Look upon it as one long letter the story of my first leave in "furrin parts". Tomorrow then and until then love to all.


Kal Jun MDCDXLIV
[ May 21st 1944 ]
[Lebanon SOE]


To continue the saga, I, we, talked, and I was bidden to go to Damascus and stay chez Piere with his friend already mentioned. Another American car rolled up so we lay in the road and it had to stop. Another charming Colonel gave me a lift to Damascus and we met a couple of the Roosevelt clan – the late President, not the present President – at least his son or cousin or fifty first cousin.

Damascus is a beautiful city, the city of dreaming Minarets – the camp was 12 miles outside in the fertile plain, bounded by the desert on one side and Hermon on part of t'other, Palestine to the South. But George Dickie Clark was out visiting a local chieftain, Suzerain of the Jebel Druze, who gave the French so much trouble not long ago.

So leaving an introductory note explaining myself I went back to Damascus and wandered through the long straight narrow streets, visited the silk market and the silver market, drank Turkish coffee – many cups, with a most pleasant old Arab

– we talked most amiably and he recited parts of the Koran to me. I smoked a Hubble Bubble, a Chibuque, a Hookah, or what you will – more pleasant than an ordinary pipe and I nearly bought one – and so in the evening I Occidentalised myself and returned to that seat of culture and refinement the Officer's Club, where, meeting a couple of acquaintances at the bar, we dined and saw a bad, very bad flick.

It is morning now, and my room mate is sound asleep, lying fully dressed on his bed – the thought of a long journey ahead of him made him feel too tired to even undress – split infinitive – I go out and buy a book to share my breakfast with. It is Galsworthy, who would certainly disapprove of being read at the breakfast table. Then I am rung up by Dickie Clark who will lunch with me at one o'clock. So in the meantime the barber at the Orient Palace Hotel has the honour of my patronage – and charges me £2. Luckily the pound here is worth 2/2d. All the money here is paper, masses of it notes ranging from £50 to 5 piastres. It can be used for money or lavatory paper. I will continue again in another letter after tea.

May 21st 1944
[Lebanon SOE]

Nothing else did I buy as I thought I had the most beautiful cloth vended, but if I ever return – as I hope to do – to the street called Straight, then will I buy more of the same cloth, and perhaps a scimitar for David and for Lalla a precious stone.

I returned with George and my small pack to their camp, set in the barren land near the foot hills of Hermon; Did you know that Hermon is

traditionally the scene of the Transfiguration –
'tho many say Tabor south in Palestine. At a later
hour, as night fell and it grew cool, we returned to
Damascus – drank English whisky – rather Scotch
– and ate sausages and fried eggs – a good meal –
and then repaired to the night club – so called – the
pride of Damascus and fritterer away of Damascene
fortunes. Charges excessive but we drank only
beer. A Husky limbed and dusky voiced Negress
was Queen of the Cabaret. She danced beautifully
and drank like a fish – but not with me.

At midnight we went to a café and drank café
a la Turque – is that correct? Anyway Turkish
coffee which I love. Then home we raced and
through the rain in an open Jeep. Next morning
I had the exquisite pleasure of hearing the other
Officers doing PT at 6 o'clock while I lay in bed
and consumed large quantities of tea. Never have
I felt better.

This day – it was a Tuesday – I had to return to
Beirut for the assembling of the course. Luckily my
friends had a car going in on duty so the journey
was easily made – myself driving for 58 kilometres.
Up in the mountains a dense mist lay – strato
cumulus, wet and cold, but when we reached the
seaboard all was sun and hot again. That night
in the mule mess we played Bridge and I won a
Pound Syrian.

Next day we all departed North to the camp
which is my residence for three weeks. The sea to
the west – to the East the fine range of the Cedars
of Lebanon – 8000 feet above us and snow capped.
We live under the olive trees in a land of great
fertility and I am the servant of a Mule. For him
I arise at 5:30 am – to him I am nothing, by him
I am likely to suffer great injury, with him I shall
march strenuously, from him kicks – not ha'pence.

Part of the training for SOE was learning how to handle mules, which were important beasts of burden in rough mountainous territory, and sometimes sources of food. The following letters describe the mule course. The mule poem was written over two of the letters.

May 23rd 1944
[Lebanon SOE]

I had a fine letter of thanks from the Div Commander of 10th Indian Div eulogising my efforts. So I am now satisfied – and the Captaincy will come along in due course – 'tho of course I should never have shed it.

Were you no doubt surprised to hear of me as a muleteer? Three weeks the course lasts. After this we have at least two more courses, possibly three.

We run our own mess here; very free and easy – we don't dress up at all. All day I wear nothing but a pair of shorts and a pair of boots. I am very brown and getting browner every day. In the afternoons alternately we bathe in the sea, and ride – this afternoon I rode and we cantered through and down the fine river up to the stirrups in rushing water which was fun. The country is magnificent – snow still on the Leban Range.

Our American has left us – we are all very sorry. He has done much to enhance our opinions of our allies. He was a nice fellow. I have written more to "Mules on the Mountain". What tripe!-however it occupies my evenings.

# MULES ON THE MOUNTAIN
Or
Regnum Mulieris

Tolson, Muleteer, Loquitur


".........and the high formless mountains
Zigzagged against the sky,
Mingle with the valley sounds –
And far below, the sea; where fly
The Caignes.  My tent beneath the trees,
The olive trees, where the goats wander
With their bells, and making music
As in old France.

The ice cold mountain stream,
Runs, falls, and dreams.  In reverie
While tending mules I often pray
That I may squander, day by day,
My life beside the pebble stones
Vaguely and emotively.

Marginal in thought, and shade,
I lie, and dream because
I only hear the frogs beneath
The bridge below the snows.

This land of spice and cedar wood
Of lapis  lazuli and ancient laughter
Where no King's ransom bought a beggar's daughter,

And now the tight twisted shepherd's song
Slips like a sonnet sequence through the river.

As if from far Medina, minaretted,
God's word is still proclaimed.
A precious sliver
Of jesting fragmentary truth.
Aye aye, and tooth for tooth.


May 25th 1944
[Lebanon SOE]


Last night, unleashed for seven hours from the fantastic mule world which we inhabit waking, I dreamed I was wafted back to England in a sky chariot and deposited in the Berkeley, where I had a bath, and then met you for dinner – and afterwards home by the slow old train. Presage, image, or mere wishful thinking.

Yesterday we held a race meeting, mules only – a successful meeting – with a steeple chase for students attending the course.

How kind I was to my mule – He is called by me "Titus" after the destroyer of the Temple, the ravager of Jerusalem – all that day; and with what fear I mounted his serrated and jagged back – we rode without saddles bare backed with a bridle.

Luckily, my mule refused the first jump so I was unable to finish the race – but it was great fun. The Cypriots love it. How no one was killed I don't know – I rode home on Titus, canter and trot, and he was amenable to my half-hearted discipline. Tomorrow we have a short route march with mules

– not more than 20 miles I gather – I hope.

Mule naming is a great game we have in our ranks a "Montgomery", a "Maclennagan" – called after the CO on our last course – a "Claudius", "Rosy" a mare, "Samuel" also curiously enough a mare.

It is a lovely evening now, cool, already dark, and the young crescent moon. Noises, only the swift mountain stream and numberless frogs; how Aristophanes would have rejoiced in this place.

May 27th 1944

Yesterday across country we tracked with our mules – two of us, fault of the mules, lost the others – we had a grand time wandering off by ourselves; we took photographs which I will send.

May 28th 1944

This evening we played Bridge. I lost three boxes of matches ie 15 piastres at 5 piastres a hundred. Have you read any Virginia Woolf – If not – try and get hold of The Waves – or To The Lighthouse, or Mrs Dalloway – you will like them. No more now – tomorrow we go on a 4 day exercise with mules starting at four in the morning.

June 1st 1944
[Lebanon SOE]

Yesterday beneath an olive tree I began a letter, but night was approaching, and the watering of mules, so I ceased and now begin again. We are returned from our four day exercise cum mules beginning at daybreak from our camp we meandered the first uphill and into the mists- the smoky scarves that seem to linger on each peak at this time of year. And so after eight leagues we rested, 4500 feet high, and the wet invisible mist made the early night clammy cold and uncomfortable.

Next morning like York's army we descended, nearly to the plains, and halted at one o'clock – an orphanage a hundred metres away – which I and another marked down as a refuge for the performing of an ablution – We washed, and stayed to dine with the head of the establishment, a most charming Catholic Priest, an Arab, he spoke French, Greek, and of course his native tongue. We haltingly exercised our ancient French.

The food was a dream, nearly all home produced, and completely Arabic in flavour and intention except for some hard boiled eggs, which I fancy were for our especial foreign benefit. He was very Francophile, and gave the best apologia for the continuance of French influence in the Levant after the war that I have ever heard from anyone. We ate until darkness covered the table and then sat out on the still roof, and the Cypriots sang to sleep their mules. They have many quaint customs, and that is the only pleasing one that I have discovered so far.

Very shortly now we return to our HQ – our next course has been suddenly cancelled. It is hard to believe it is June.

A lovely bathe this afternoon in the mountain river, O so cold – but lovely afterwards, and sunbathing with nothing on. I hope we get the photographs soon. Hope you recognise me in them.

*Richard with parents, 1940?*

*Marjorie Tolson and Richard July 1940*

*Richard's first platoon marching to Magilligan,*
*Co. Derry, 1939, CSM Cracknell on his left*

*Richard on Lake Enniskilen, April 1939*
*taken by Philip Harris*

*Lake Tiberius, May 1944*

*l to r: Richard, Jack Murow, Peter Lee, Jim Gail, Jim Beatt, Mike Lycett ~ The Lebanon, 1944*

*Porzus: looking across to Monty Joannes, the dropping ground in 1944. Stremitz is down the valley to the right of the photo*

*?, Paul Brietsche, ?, and Richard*

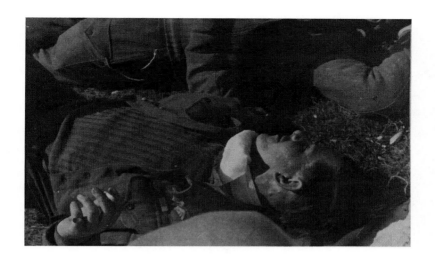

*Thank God for a cigarette*

*1944 in N Italy ~ Richard, Paul Brietsche, Victor Gozzer*

*Major Tilman, Dec. 3rd 1944*

*Paul, Dick, Norman, Pauline, Milo, Gemma, Major, Victor ~*
*November 1944*

*Malta 1947*

*Dicky Johnsen, Cpl. Sergent, Richard Tolson*
*Malta, April 1947*

*Jordan, Royal Sussex and Union flags, Aquaba*

*After the fire, Aquaba, June 1950*

*Richard Tolson, right, playing chess, Port Said, 1952*

*May 1951 ~ Mt. Sinai 'The Hand of God"*

# 11

## From Egypt to Italy

The SOE training in Palestine was over, but some more was still to come, first in Egypt and later in Italy. Italy had surrendered in September 1943, and by the end of the year the allies had occupied the country south of Naples. The North was still held by the Germans, and Mussolini remained there as a puppet ruler. The north was gained by the Allies only very slowly, with many hard fought battles, such as those at Monte Cassino and Anzio. Richard transferred from Egypt to Italy in July 1944. He was based near Bari, where parachute training took place. He was preparing to join the Italian Partisans in North East Italy.

In June 1944 the war in Europe had taken a new turn. On the 6th of that month, D-Day, the Allies invaded France in the Normandy peninsula, and began the long advance across Northern Europe. Richard's brother David, a Gunner, landed on Gold beach on D-Day +2.

June 11th 1944

[Egypt]

Today we have rejoiced officially in HM's birthday by arriving weary and travel stained at our HQ – the journey from Syria was energetic and uncomfortable. By chicanery only, did two of our party – I was one – gain 1st class seats with 2nd class tickets. Officially there is no difference and an Officer may travel first or second class – in actual fact there is the same difference as between purgatory and hell, or what we might imagine it to be. Both bad, but one can be suffered knowing you probably deserved it, and to endure the other induces an enraged resentment.

The course ended without a kick and last Sunday we repaired from Tripoli to Beirut to await our train passage hither.

I am with two days to squander, and dreaming Damascuswards I find myself there; four hours by the clock – two minutes in the imagination. Peter is left, only two days before and I stay at the "Cercle des Officiers" far nicer than the British Officer's club.

I dined alone that night, it is late and delicately cool  One by one the diners depart and the small flower vase form up on the fountain side. Little desolate check tables, green and yellow, with black zebra stripes and the reproach of red wine in stains. But somehow spontaneity survives, and the large hippodromic windows opposite, with protractor-like curved ends, throw a shadow of light – and the mind peoples an otherwise empty hall beyond.

The wine in my glass splutters, and goes out. I dine alone in short trousers, and because of them cannot go out to see the Dervishes who will be dancing – flaunting the near full moon. So I will go to bed in a large French feather bed – goose feather bed, I trust – and the trams outside pulverise the paving stones of the street.

Now it is yesterday and we follow Alexander down the coast – Sidon surrenders, Tyre is stubborn, Accra is sacked, Athleit is not yet built. But Joppa, Ashdod, and Gaza all fall to the conqueror, to Alexander, to the Palestine railway, and crossing Sinai by night, today we are in – well, the city that commands the cradle of the world. The post is just arrived – six letters from you – will write tomorrow.

148

June 12th 1944
[Egypt]

Here then we are still and thank you for your letters
rolling in. So far seven are arrived here the latest in
date of paring June 2nd – which is admirably quick.

I like very much the Sanscrit invocation – it
reminds me of T.E.Lawrence's story of the old
Arab who with "hewn face of great power and
weariness", sat down beside a pool wherein was
Lawrence lying – and he peered forward and at last
seemed content as he "groaned", "The love is from
God; and of God; and towards God".

We are still at this dump although having an
enjoyable time would be glad to get cracking away
from the big city. Every morning, which is most
pleasant I go with someone to Gezira and we bathe
all morning and afternoon and eat a small picnic
lunch on the terrace. Sometimes I watch the cricket,
and the number of chaps I've met in the last few
days – extraordinary. On Saturday night I dined
with Brigadier James and his G.I., at the Turf Club
– a most charming evening – and I think it will
prove most helpful in the recovery of the pay they
stole from me over dropping the temporary rank.

How hot and dull and cramped this place
is after Lebanon. There we had hawks, eagles,
cedar trees and mountain streams, here we have
the hoopoo bird, what looks like, but isn't, the
ylangylang tree, and of course a swimming pool.

I feel sure David will be all right in this messy
business. I would I were tit for tatting in France –
1940 was a mess up – but this time the whip is in
the right hands. No Zoar for Jerry, as for us, then.

June 16ᵗʰ 1944
[Egypt]

I write by ordinary mail, in order to include a photograph of myself – rather an unusual angle I'm afraid, unrecognisable I expect but anyway it is a photograph taken on or about the 10ᵗʰ of May, and shows myself wading out into the Sea of Gallilee South of Tiberias. Opposite are the Trans Jordanian hills, and the lake is a good 300 feet below sea level. It was our first, and best, bathe this year; a previous letter, I think, refers. I will let you have the mule photographs as soon as possible. Last night tobacco arrived from Hamilton House – I write immediately.

This is a very dull and uninteresting letter, but then this is a very hot, dull, and uninteresting place. Hope David is corresponding regularly, and everyone well at home.

June 23ʳᵈ 1944
[Egypt]

I hope for one from you tonight, but must get this off before the afternoon post. It is really too hot to be pleasant now, so have abandoned Gezira for a couple of days and stay indoors. Has the letter with the photograph arrived yet?

I have been playing quite a bit of bridge in the evenings and am becoming very scientific, practicing the Culbertson convention and counting up my hand correctly. However I am still hopeless when I get a bad hand, and am inclined to underbid.

I had a long talk with Uncle B the other day – said he had seen my report which was very good and was very pleased with what I was doing. My Captaincy is coming through as from March 10<sup>th</sup>.

For the last five days I've been engrossed in the Seven Pillars of Wisdom, which before I never could read. It is a wonderful book, and having recently read all his letters and Doughty's Arabia Deserta I am enjoying it thoroughly.

The Damascus brocade will arrive shortly I trust. I think I have a safe way of sending it to you. I also enclose a Bethlehem New Testament with odds and ends of postcards of Places visited. This afternoon I am going to a cinema to see a comedy – probably go to sleep.

With love to all, and thoughts for David's safe return.

June 25<sup>th</sup> 1944

[Egypt]

As I thought, two letters arrived from you the evening after I posted my last. Very glad to get all the news, and that David is going strong. Here, so far, I have lead a very marginal life and have always many thoughts for you and him, especially now.

I forgot to send Uncle Bernard's love when I last wrote, which I do now. It is possible that you may have to wait a little longer for my next letter – but don't worry, the delay will not be long, and I may have a new address for you to write to 'tho this address will always find me in the long run. So far no shaving soap, or Blackwoods, due I'm afraid to my many moves. I think it would be well to stop sending Blackwoods as I have had none since February. I still hope the shaving soap will turn up, 'tho I still go strongly on the last parcel.

I have finished the 7 Pillars and am now rereading it very carefully, or trying to, for everyone here wants to borrow it. I have a very bad summer cold which should pass in a day or two. It was cooler today – and a letter from Aunt G this evening requesting one from me at my pleasure – I think I wrote a fortnight ago but can't be sure. However!!!!

I see no reason why, if we like the place, we should not settle down between the Chilterns and Aylesbury – unless the house owners are repulsive and will not accommodate us. But Devon sounds nice though 200 miles away. Why not the West Indies, and from there I can ply a lucrative trade in guns and dope to the Banda Orientale. Of course I should have to send in my papers first but I do not feel enamoured of the army any more – How right you were – ? !!!! [1]

The Royal Sussex Regiment
M.E. 56 C.M.F.
[Italy -South]

July 4th 1944

As you can perhaps guess we are now in Italy – arriving a short time ago after a most pleasant voyage with no excitement of any description – on the way the sea was very blue, very calm, and the food on board very good; and that is really the sum total of the voyage as it concerned me. We played bridge every evening and I held the most appalling cards, and lost about a quid.

Most unattached Officers – without a party of men to look after – were given some duty, and I was detailed to conduct, compose and occasionally confound, a party of Italian diplomats returning to their native land from Turkey. There was one charming Naval Commander who naively told me that he had been sent to Turkey to recover his nerves. He had been stationed at Taranto so he had ample opportunity to lose them. The head of the mission had been Consul General in London up to 1939. Luckily they could all speak English.

We live in a typical Italian villa, which presents a brave front to the world, but is appallingly insanitary, at least by English standards. The food seems good, no messing charges, but eggs, if you want them, are 9p a piece. Vin ordinaire diluted with lemonade or water seems to be the normal drink, and it is quite amiable. We enjoy very pleasant sea bathing, a small land locked cove, all rocks, no sand. The open shore is reputedly dangerous. But you can dive straight in and the water is very warm – as warm, I think, as Galillee.


July 15th 1944
[Italy – South]


Six slow days and no news to tell. I was delighted to get yours of the 22/23rd; didn't think it would catch up so quickly. I'm afraid I have not made myself very clear as to what I am doing now, but that is chiefly due to security. I am not with the Regiment at all, but with an organisation called Force 133; it has different names in different parts of the world. Of course I still belong to the Royal Sussex. Uncle B recommended me for this, when I saw him last March.

Colonel James is now on the GHQ staff in Cairo, and was head of the department that was ultimately responsible for my Battle School. Thus it was that I went to see him about my third pip.

I hope you will receive my parcel soon. It will be posted in England – safer, I think, and should be followed up by a visit from a chap called Eric Newlyn, he is in this firm, and will tell you about our few weeks in Cairo. He is a subaltern in the Sappers. He is going home to get married, so will probably be in a bit of a dither – still he promised to go and see you.

Hope you have had a lot more letters from David by now. Sure he will look after himself all right. The hills here look just like the Chilterns from the monument, and going southwards, except of course for the sea. Take care of yourselves.

July 15th 1944
[Italy – South]

Just a line by sea mail in order to enclose a couple of mule photographs. I have written on the back the names. They are all fellows in the same show as self. Last night we celebrated genially the 14th Juillet. [2] We experienced yesterday the first rain I have met with for some months, it turned surprisingly cold and we even wore cardigans and woolly waistcoats in the evening.

Your letter addressed to Cairo arrived two days ago (with the rain) how welcome. At the time you write I was on board ship – 'tho I must confess that Lawrence has impressed me so much that I know chunks of it almost by heart. Everyone is trying to borrow it and I don't get a chance to study him as I would like to.

My particular half section on the mule course was Lee, third from the left in the larger photograph. His mule (Rosie) the rather dumb looking animal with an eye fringe, and mine, on whose neck, or rather withers, my hand rests, got on very well together.


July 22nd 1944

[Italy – South]


Some days I'm afraid since I wrote – but I have been away on a course. I expect daily now to hear from you at this address. But the mail doesn't appear to be too good at present for anyone.

I have procured two kilos of almonds which I am sending as soon as I can get a decent box. They should come in handy for Christmas, which already seems to be approaching quickly.

I'm sorry I heard about the cousin in Cairo too late to be able to see him it would have been very interesting meeting him. It is the hottest year there for a long time and it is getting hotter every day here. Flies are pretty terrible but the mosquito nets keep them off at night.

I have just finished my parachute training and am now fully qualified in that gentle art. It is a bit scarifying at first, but nothing in it, and as safe as houses. I have done four jumps, one of them at night and had beautiful landings each time; of course it was also my first flying experience, but being a bit preoccupied with the jumping, I just never had time to think that it was the first time I had left terra firma. The monstrous peace and bliss that you feel drifting silently down is accentuated by having left the noise inside the plane, and just passed through the slip stream, a charybdis of seething air.

I'm not likely to jump again for ages, so don't go worrying and thinking I'm hopping out of planes all day every day – and as I say it safer than driving a car down the Portsmouth Road in peace time – there's much more room.


## PARACHUTING

You ask me, what is the sensation
When, like a god descending,
Flung from a chariot of high moving cloud
I slowly earthwards drift. I hear the sounds
Of  torrents in the rushing wind which cleaves
The senses launched in space, and sends
My body safe, as on shore seeking waves;
Then suddenly, as if the nearing sands
Have satisfied the fury, gentleness
Is come upon me; floating on calm waters
I look and see the land.
Not with mortal eyes, but far seeing;
No detail here; but all the earth is saying
"This is the larger beauty, look on this".
And then the ground is risen, and the vision
Fades, I must forget
The transient passage when I was a god.
And I am glad to touch the common earth
Which is my life, and will be mine in death.

# 12

## Richard's Diary of his months with the Partisans

Entirely against regulations, Richard kept a diary of his experiences with the Italian Partisans. I believe many soldiers disobeyed the instructions. The diary was written in pencil on flimsy blue paper, and was tucked into a wallet. With it were two poems.

From the base in South Italy, Richard was parachuted in to the North East, landing near the border with Yugoslavia. He was dropped to the wrong place, but fortunately to friends. He was sent as a British liaison officer, with a radio operator, to give support to the Partisan attempts at sabotage. The main support was in the form of air drops of weapons and other supplies. The DZ, or dropping zone, is often referred to. The failure of drops was a continual frustration; successful drops were greeted with joy. Although Richard parachuted in on September 19th 1944, the diary does not begin until October. The two following passages describe something of the first month, and explain some of the terms used.

### Introduction to the war diary [written 1991]

Our briefing, before the first of three attempted sorties, had been evasive and imprecise – lots of hopefulness, and, almost, optimism – but we were not, at the end of it, so certain as to what our role would be.

From Brindisi, then, two quite impossible attempts were made to land somewhere north- east of Udine. A multiplicity of fire signals in the plain but no sign on the hills beyond.. And besides, the pilots and crew were impatient to return to a dance at their base.

The third attempt was from Bari: a black night, no moon at all. The flight, once we were over the Veneto, above a marvellous sea of cloud. Then, searching from the broad gleam of the River Tagliamento Eastwards, lights were found. Our lights, someone supposed. We got ready to jump, hooked up on the strong point of the wretched old plane.

It was my job to see everyone out, and jump on the second time round, alone, followed by the kit. All went quite well and we landed among friends on Monte Johanaz, not far from the little village of Canebola.

We jumped from a much lower ceiling than I had supposed and I was still adjusting my goggles when I made a perfect landing on the side of the mountain.

Next morning, the little hills perfect, autumnal – what a change from bloated Bari and Brindisi.

## September 19th – October 28th

*The group of partisans and British Officers gathered at Canebola. Hedley Vincent was the senior British Officer. Almost immediately a* rastrellamento *occurred. This was the term given to a German attack, literally a "raking through", forcing the Partisans to flee. Germans threatened from all sides, and Richard with Tom Rowarth and Laybourne, the radio operator, and Piave,[1] a Partisan, headed west across the Tagliamento river. The water was high and it was a long wade with baggage.*

*They reached Trasaghis on the west bank where a baby girl had just been born, and Richard gave his parachute, with its precious silk, to the infant. Richard was heading for Tramonti, the place where he was supposed to have landed. He stayed there briefly before moving to Clauzetto, which is where his diary begins.*

*The Partisans did not use their real names, but each had a* nome di guerra, *and many are named in the diary. There were two Partisan factions. On one side were the*

*Garibaldini, committed communists. On the other were the Osoppo, who were more right-wing. Both were intensely anti-fascist, and many men joined the Partisans who had no particular allegiance to either faction.*

*Apart from the initial rastrellamento, there were two more major ones to come. One occurred when the Cossacks attacked Tramonti, and another when Richard had trekked further West to join Paul Brieitche, one of the British Officers. It happened in deep snow, and was the most serious conflict of Richard's time in North Italy.*

### Diary October 1944 – February 1945

As I write I am seated in the low kitchen of an old farmhouse overlooking the plain that stretches from Alp to Appenine. The year is in late October, mists have hung about our heads for the last ten days and the snow is settling firmly and whitely lower and lower down towards the plain. The rivers, too, show great increase, for rain has been heavy and continuous, and their straightness lies white, stretched across the plain below, disappearing into the haze that wreathes the Adriatic shore.

Down on the plain the Germans await their last winter of war in Italy. The Patriots have re-occupied positions from which ten days ago they were forced to withdraw, and from which the enemy, in his turn, has retired. The hills are unsympathetic towards the traditional enemy, who may advance to burn and kill, but cannot hold a place there for long.

I am attached to the Head Quarters of the "Gruppo Sud" of the Division Garibaldi-Osoppo "Friuli" with a radio set and Italian operator, formerly of the Italian Airforce, who rejoices in the nome di guerra of Dynamo. So far we have been unable to contact our parent station, but Dynamo remains hopeful, and I shall send him to Tramonti tomorrow if we do not transmit tonight.

The group Commander is a young man who is called Battisti; a large man with a mass of curly hair and a dark beard. Always cheerful with a great love for music, which incessantly we compare humming tune for tune, he is an ardent communist, and possesses one red shirt, and no other clothes worth speaking of. He talks quietly, with a slight stammer, but dominates any company in which he is found. His brother in arms, and peer, is Sergio, the Group Political commissario, who is small, with an auburn beard and very steady, sincere eyes. He is only twenty one, but has suffered prison for his political convictions. We speak French together, and he has an equal love of France with me. Their staff consists of two boys aged about eighteen, one of whom does the typewriting, and the other the cooking. They both love American or 'English' tobacco, and do not mind asking for it.

Today we have suffered two bits of good fortune; some tobacco arrived from somewhere this morning, and some wine is rumoured to be arriving this afternoon. Yesterday they captured two German lorry loads of bombs and ammunition, and also enough cloth to make a uniform overall for the whole division. The stuff is blue but that does not appear to trouble their political consciences.

Both leaders spend any spare time in reading and writing political treatises, and have a large book which contains the texts of Magna Carta, the Petition of Right, the Bill of Rights, the Act of Settlement, the Declaration of Independence, the Rights of Man, and other liberal charters. These are read, reread, and thoroughly explored, and produced at length in innumerable articles – for the Party paper. Their respect for our political freedoms in the past is only equalled by their admiration for Russia and their desire for the Communist International.

My library here contains three French books. One is "Paul & Virginia" which I read at school, but find very pleasant now; another is Flaubert's "Salammbo" which I shall shortly begin, and the third is a selection of D.H. Lawrence's letters translated, with an introduction, by Aldous Huxley. At any rate my French is improving, if not my Italian. Unfortunately I left my Seven Pillars of Wisdom at Tramonti, but hope to regain it soon.

We have two meals a day, with erzatz coffee in the morning. However, it seems plenty, and I eke out the coffee with a tin of marmalade, instead of dipping my roll into the coffee. When the marmalade is finished I have one tin of bacon, and after that I too shall have to dip with the rest.

The local village is Clauzetto, where you can get a haircut, and a watch repaired, but not buy a pipe. The local doctor keeps a good brand of Italian cognac, of which we partake when I visit him with Battisti.

The Division boasts a priest, Don Giulio, who is very pleasant, and speaks French. But it is obvious that Italian communists can reconcile God with their political beliefs; on the other hand not half of the Garibaldini are communist, but just patriots who have joined up to fight the enemy of Church and Communism alike.

A great joy here is my small radio, RBZ, and everyone eagerly listens to the news from Radio London. At the beginning of this news we also get the messagi speciali which inform us whether we will get a drop tonight or not; so I also have good reason to listen.

Today the allied armies are on the verge of taking Mussolini's birth place, and coupled with the fact that it is the anniversary of the March on Rome, it gives great delight to the patriots. They won't be content until Musso goes to the wall in the literal sense of the phrase.

Half past three, miserably cold and wet outside, but the wine has just arrived, and is on the table. This is at least a sensible country in regard to drinking. The wine is red and raw, this year's vintage, and is improved with sugar, but it is the first for a week, and therefore doubly grateful.

Our situation here is pleasant. To the south the plains, as far as eye can see, with the Tagliamento and Meduna running straight down from the hills to an eventual junction. To the north is Mt Rosso, not yet snow covered but rising sheer and forbidding from our little valley: To the west Mt Ciaurlec and to the east Mt Pala, which is occupied by an Osoppo Brigade. One kilometre south is Clauzetto, our metropolis.

The other half of the 'Unified' command resides in Campone, a village north of Mt Ciaurlec, and distant about 10kms from here. This is Carlo of the Osoppo a regular Italian Officer, who unfortunately does not hit it off with Battisti, and so lives as far away as possible, with Roncioni, Commander of the 4th Osoppo Brigade a courteous and hospitable gentleman, and I wish Carlo was like him. Carlo resembles exactly Louis XI of France in my imagination – sly peering eyes, hooked nose and bald head. He calls me his "cher ami" but has never helped as Battisti does. I am trying to get him replaced by Roncioni who gets on very well with Battisti, and Corrado, the Garibaldi 'Tagliamento' Brigade Commander, who also has his HQ at Campone.

The South Group is made up of four Brigades : two Garibaldi – Tagliamento and Picelli – and two Osoppo, the 3rd and 4th. Dissension between them is unfortunately considerable, and the Osoppo have been making capital out of the last engagement, in which they say, the Garibaldi ran away in disorder, leaving the Osoppo to bear the brunt of the action.

If only Base would listen to our demands for arms and ammo the Germans could never get a foothold in the hills, which will be of vital importance when the retreat into Austria begins. Ninci, the Garibaldi Divisional Commander was going out in a Lysander to put the case to the High Command, but the enemy rastrellamento[2] ended in the loss of the field, and now that we have it back the weather has turned vile, at least rather like a wet October afternoon in England – but there is no game of rugger this afternoon, followed by tea and hot buttered scones, and lashings of good honest beer in the pub afterwards. Saturday afternoon, but what a difference.

Sudden interruption – Enemy Cossack Troops are reported to be in S. Francesco which is 10 kms away, and held by Garibaldini. We have packed up the radio and all our kit, and are ready, if necessary, to flit. The old woman in whose house I have a room is nearly in tears and thinks it will be burned to the ground. But we will leave no trace of our lodgement. I don't particularly like the idea of running tonight, its started to rain again, and the radio makes it no joke. Oh for arms and ammo. However, it may not be as bad as we think.

*Sunday the 29ᵗʰ* October, and very cold with a promise of more rain. Had a very good night in spite of the alarming news that 1500 Cossack and German troops were on the road to S. Francesco, using the civilian population as shields, and meeting no opposition. Sergio returned from Div HQ last night after an annoying journey during which he had to carry the car across the Meduna as the bridge has been destroyed, and finally had to walk from Campone as the car broke down – and no wonder, the way its treated.

This morning the news is much better; the enemy having dwindled to 250 men and a Battalion of the Picelli Brigade is standing in their path on the other side of S. Francesco. News from Div HQ is that Ninci and Andrea, Div Cmdr and Commissario of the Garibaldi, have gone off to Carnia to shoot or otherwise encourage the leaders who failed up there early this month. Plauto, Commissario of the Osoppo, is going to Rome, if the Lysander materialises, instead of Ninci; and Manfred, the Austrian Section BLO is going out as well. No news of Tom or the rest of the mission, so presumably all's well. Hope he's getting my sitreps.

*30th October.* Last night the alarm having somewhat abated, Battisti and I walked down to Clauzetto after supper to call on the Doctor and his wife. Very charming with two small children, we played silly games and drank tea with cognac, and afterwards cognac alone with plenty of roasted chestnuts. We departed at midnight, clear and cold, and sang all the way home. The Lysander landed at Tramonti yesterday and we eagerly await news of who is going, or has gone out. The Partizans apparently fired on the Lysander as it came down, but as usual didn't hit anything.

The RAF bombed the bridge at Pinzano yesterday morning but they didn't hit it either. Today heavy rain but seems to be clearing up a bit now at 11 o'clock. I hope the Lysander has brought our mail. I don't think we shall get up to San Francesco now, as the bridge has not been repaired and Battisti not yet returned. Dynamo has procured another battery for the radio, so we will be able to keep up regular transmissions, and has now gone off to Tramonti to confabulate with Laybourne and if possible bring back the hand charger, some tobacco, and mail, if any.

The letters of D.H. Lawrence were most interesting, and I must read some of his books on my return. I have copied out some of his reflections on political ideals, which should please Sergio – 'tho Lawrence appears to have been no communist in the accepted sense of the word, but an independent and sincere idealist who could never have transmuted his thoughts into action.

It is interesting to see that he had no faith in Democracy as he knew it and in fact prophesied an English revolution in 1925, which nearly came to pass. That prophesy was made in 1915, and he said "après la guerre, l'âme de tous les êtres sera si mutilée, si blessée, qu'il est affreux d'y penser. Et le nouvel espoir sera dans une vie ou la lutte ne soit pas pour l'argent ou la puissance, mais pour la liberté individuelle, et l'effort commun vers le bien.'

This is more vastly true today, for the war is on a vaster scale; but we must remember that it applies equally to our enemy, especially the naughty little boy of Europe, who given the chance, may grow to be an upright and honest citizen of the World. If the patriots of Italy have their way, Italy will be lost to the world for many years, as they are resolved to eliminate, to snuff out, every single man who has had any part in or of the Fascist Republic since the armistice.

I was talking to an intelligent Garibaldini yesterday and he said that all, however much or little they were involved, must be done away with, down to the lowest forcibly conscripted man. This sounds absurd, but it is their real and avowed intention, and shows that, in spite of their waffle of freedom of thought and action, they have all got the fascist complex. Freedom of thought means only freedom to think as I think, or else the rope. The most encouraging words I have heard were from Tacito of the Osoppo who remarked that he hoped to God the English would stay to regulate and guide affairs after the war – a country with no political perspective, and envy and malice towards all, including their own countrymen who think differently.

It is now tea time, and we have taken a dish of tea, the wine is on the table and sausages of a kind frizzling on the fire, for the benefit of divers types who have just arrived. All very pleasant; but heaven help Italy if one in ten of them have any say in the moulding of their country after the war. Battisti and Sergio are definitely outstanding, are I think, bigger men than Ninci or Andrea, and will probably make their mark in politics afterwards, as they are both, apparently, determined to do.

Today the Tagliamento Battalion is taking over the front line from the Sozzi, whose footwear will not stand up to active service. It is literally true that one in ten has no footwear at all, and half go about in the Italian equivalent of carpet slippers. A report has just come in saying that the Germans have now moved up into the hills to the South at Forgaria, which is about 4 kms ESE of Clauzetto. This means that they are menacing our positions on the road, which runs due North and South through the hills to join the upper Tagliamento Valley, and we are approximately in the middle; they may intend joining forces at Pielungo and then push West down past Campone to the Meduna Valley, Redona and Tramonti; in which case we shall probably be on the move very shortly. Sergio is bringing me a Sitrep immediately. Weather has stopped all action on the army fronts; I wish they'd stop here for a night.

*31st October.* The North front appears to be stabilised for the present, as the enemy have withdrawn to Pozzis and our troops have made a corresponding advance. On the

South front all troops have withdrawn to the line of the Road Vito d'Asio – Clauzetto, and we await developments.

This morning for petit dejeuner we had a little bacon, tinned, and rolls, washed down with wine and hot fresh milk. A curious mixture but appetising.

Today is our forty second day with the Partizans and a great deal seems to have happened since we dropped at Canebola near Attimis on the night of September 19th. The German rastrellamento started over there three days after we left and Hedley has been on the run since then and the Division broken up. Most of the Garibaldini in that area have gone over to the Slovenes. Here the Germans have occupied the whole of the Tagliamento valley, occupied Ampezzo, the capital of the liberated territory, and pushed up from the North and South through the Meduna valley, which forced us to take to the hills on October 18th. When the Cossacks left Tramonti I came over here to liase with the Gruppo Sud on October 25th.

This afternoon for the first time in a week there is a blue sky visible. Our planes have been bombing some place on the plain since two o'clock this afternoon. Perhaps having another go at the Bridge near Pinzano. No fresh news this evening, activity on both our fronts being very light.

Today is *November 2nd.* Had no time to write anything yesterday, as we were out all day visiting Positions. etc. We started off by visiting Anduins, the most easterly of the Positions yet getatable by road. A lively battle was raging along the front, the Germans using mortars, and our chaps MG's and Carbines. We could see the Hun cautiously advancing along the road to Forgaria, which we eventually occupied about eleven thirty, together with two hills which dominate the Plain, the two roads from the South, and Anduins and Vito d'Asio. Towards the end enemy mortar fire was dropping quite close to us at Anduins.

While at Anduins I met the Commandant and 2 in command of the Embryo Battalion., "Karl Marx", which will be composed solely of Germans. Its purpose is firstly

166

propaganda value, and secondly, to be used eventually in Austria, 'tho I greatly doubt this. They were both exceedingly pleasant, and spoke, but could not well understand, English. The Commandant was a Luftwaffe officer and the 2 in command rejoices in the name of 'Jackie'. They were on their way to Tramonti where the Battalion is forming.

On the way back I saw Miro, Commander of the 3rd Osoppo Battalion. He is a difficult customer, a time server and insincere, but quite efficient, I think. I got all his new dispositions and then had to listen while he and Sergio, who dislikes him, discussed the interesting question of the Unified Command. After that we visited Elio at his pub, had a good view of his new detachment positions, and also a remarkably fine bottle of vermouth.

We lunched at Clauzetto, and then went on to Campone, where I wrote a despatch for Tom, and saw Roncioni, Commandant of 4th Osoppo, who begged for more ammunition, and wanted to send a letter regarding the situation to Marshall Messe, whom he knows. I said it might be possible per radio. It was nearly six by the time we returned to Pradis, and had a good supper before going down with Battisti to the Doctors for a little light relief. The electric light had failed in Clauzetto, but by candlelight we ate a delicious cake, home made, and drank wine, very pale and light, followed by roast chestnuts and cognac. We walked home in the pouring rain under one umbrella.

*November 2nd* is a day of mourning for the dead in Italy, and wherever we went yesterday there were great processions to the little cemetery. An unnecessary institution of holy church I think, and very pitiful to see. All black, nothing but black dresses and veils, except the children.

Today it is pelting again, and I am glad I decided to wait until tomorrow before returning to Tramonti. I can just get the latest information as regards our own and enemy positions. I am going to see Miro now. There is a possible DZ at Pradis di Sotto, rather too many trees, but it will serve if needed. Mt. Prat is too far away, and is anyway out of the question with the Germans in Forgaria.

I called at 3rd Brigade HQ but Miro and Vico were out. However, I collected all the necessary information from Eugenio. My courier of last night, who will return with me is a Pole, who speaks only German besides, and it is a little difficult at times. He is very very grave and polite; his hair incredibly long and silky. He escaped from a concentration camp at Bolzano. The wine has just run out, but luckily I have a little Grappa left.

It is curious to reflect on the unreality of our life; of our life as Englishmen among the Italians. One is happy enough, I suppose, in a flat sort of way; flattened by the weight of five war years, and now seeing that war through a looking glass and the Fascist press. Our work room and living room is the kitchen of this old house. It is very small with two wide and deep set windows looking south and west. The atmosphere is always the same; our food cooking, our socks drying, and the harsh smell of Italian tobacco.

When it is dark, an oil lamp suspended from one of the whitewashed wooden beams, gives a friendly exclusive light, dismissing in shadow the bare white walls, the stone floor, our littered arms, and the wooden crucifix high upon the west wall. Outside the leaves are rushing on the wind, and the level greyness of the sky discloses only rain. A very mourning mood fit for the dead, whose day it is, and who alone know the hopelessness of death.

Today I went to the church with Battisti, dark and thick with incense, and black and purple draped. At the east end, ten feet high rose a catafalque on which a coffin reposed painted about with the emblems of the dead; it seemed the very Cult of Death. The monstrous innocence of these people is terrifying, and the church plays on their credulity with such sure hands, that we forget the instrument, admiring only the master's delicacy of touch, and gentle precision. This Church seems not concerned with the hereafter, nor even with our present; its sympathy and memory is solely with the past; I am sure the first dogma of the church is death.

*November 3rd.* At the conference yesterday, they have adopted my suggestion as regards the Osoppo Commander of the Grappo Sud – and now Roncioni has taken Carlo's place, and is moving up to Pradis tomorrow, so the Unified Command is coming about. Carlo is now Chief of Staff to the Command. I saw him this morning on the way to Tramonti and he seemed very pleased with life. Impossible for the car to cross the Meduna, so we had to walk across a plank and eventually get a camion into Tramonti. Found Tom, Laybourne, and Pierre at Ropa. Also the Trafalgar Day letter from home. The only one but very welcome, 'tho not much news.

*Mrs M.S. Tolson*
*Excelsior Farm*
*Stoke Mandeville*
*Nr Aylesbury*
*Bucks.*

*"Trafalgar Day"* [3]

*My Darling – here we are Oct: 21st '44 all good thoughts on it commemorating the deeds of our great men. I do hope you can celebrate it in the usual way. I posted off two little books of Poetry this week, one from Auntie K and a small leaflet from me which I thought might be of interest to you. I do hope you'll get them. I've got on order for you – Lawrence Binyon's 'Burning Leaves', its in binding again, but may take a few weeks to arrive here. I do so pray you are fit and happy, it is'nt very salubrious having no letters from you, but I'm constantly being told 'no news is good news' and it bucks me up. One keeps hoping to hear-that at least our European enemies can't cope any longer, it really beats me how they can go on.*

*My stay in Town did me quite a lot of good, and I've come home less invalidish altogether. Next weekend our students go back to London to finish their course there, so at any rate for a short time I'm going to do without them; it will be a nice change ...... I also think Lalla could do with a rest. Our nerves are rather strung up.*

*The Autumn leaves are falling heavily, the country looks a bit grim, as we are having a great deal of rain. News from David last Monday did not amount to much. He was pretty busy at the time of writing Oct. 12th, and we haven't heard since, and I think there has been much activity near where he was – he sent me his Book of Coupons, & orders for shirts boots etc: I think he gets his parcels pretty well. I wish you did, I'd so enjoy sending you your wants ....*

*Well I can't post very early today so will leave this to the last minute not that one expects much news on a Saturday. I sent John Stewart's letter round to all & sundry as Aunt G for one had complained to Lalla you never wrote! So I thought that it would stop all their talk!!*

*Well here's to the next Trafalgar Day together again – God bless you darling our thoughts & prayers constantly offered for your protection and happiness.*

*Lots of love & kisses from your loving Mummie.*

Still raining like hell, and had to find a bed in Tramonti. Have secured a room in the local pub – quite comfortable, but no wine. As usual Tom is flapping about, his incredible egoistical self. God knows what he will want me to do next. Mike is just back from Carnia and says the Partisan situation is hopeless there: he wants to go off with his mission as saboteurs and blow up bridges. Pat, McCabe, and Simon are all here preparatory to going out through Jugland in a week's time. Will they be able to cross the Tagliamento? With this rain it seems doubtful.

Very relieved to hear from home that David was going strong – last news of him dated Oct 12th. He must be in Belgium now I should think.

Nov. 4th and Mummie's birthday – Many happy returns, and may I be home for the next one. It is a perfect day, the sky a deep azure with no single cloud, and now at midday very hot. Unfortunately we are on the flap again, as Cossacks are rumoured to be approaching Tramonti through the Mountains from Pozzis. This is quite possible, and most annoying as we have just received notice of a drop tonight. We await events.

The set up here is exasperating, all the political snakes hovering around eager to corrupt mens minds.

One plane arrived at Bakersfield last night. We were all there to receive it; included in the contents were, much needed mortar and ammo, and also personal mail and 2 Blackwoods Magazines. Very welcome. Letters from home. Kitty, Maxie and my two most faithful servants, Holts and the Ottoman bank Cairo.

*10th November:* About the last few days I prefer not to write at any length. They, and Tom in particular, have been exasperating. False starts, false alarms and fruitless journeyings. On the 7th I tried to get stores through to Chiamps, and having climbed 3000 feet found the snow on the North face too deep to permit descent into Chiamps. Tonight we expect a mass drop by 37 aircraft at Chiamps. Mike Prior is up there to receive it.

*11th November:* Armistice Day – & wish it were again. The drop last night lies scattered over three Mountain ranges and will take a fortnight to collect providing the snow doesn't cover it entirely. The indifference of Div HQ now that the stuff is arrived is astonishing. Mario said that if we had another drop like that they wouldn't bother to collect it. In addition both HQ's are moving to Chievolis as they think it unsafe to stay in one place more than a fortnight, and are just moving off and leaving us to organise the pulling in of all stores.

*12th November:* An affirmative crack on the radio again last night and I was down at Tramonti until midnight but no planes arrived. A beautiful night but very cold. Slept in the Priest's house at Tramonti di Sotto. Rudolf is a very nice fellow indeed – wish I were with him.

*13th November:* Last night two planes arrived at Tramonti and dropped over an enormous area. Returning to the Hotel at Tramonti di Sopra at 1.30am this morning I was nearly knocked off my bike by a package of boots all over the bridge which crosses the Meduna. Had to go back and route out Aurelio and three men to take them in as they would have disappeared by morning. God help the RAF, they need it. This morning first snow in Tramonti. I went up to Frassaneit in the afternoon to find out how Piave is getting on. He is settled in most comfortably living at the house of our old friend, and gradually getting the stuff in.

Under four inches of snow the valleys are beautiful, with every fir tree tinselled and the delicate olive green thread of river running through turning to mauve at the edges where the pebbles and stones surface. Any more snow will ruin our chances of recovering the remaining containers, and at Chiamps it is already over knee high.

*15th November:* 2 inches of snow fell last night, and the day is horribly wet and cold. The river shows definite increase and is formidable to cross in the narrow parts. Tom now wishes me to start an officers training school at Pradis, which is a good idea, but I would rather go over to Paul Brietsche and let Pat do that job. It won't last long I know very well, and Tom will be for ever interfering. If I can get away from this frightful overwhelming egotism of his I shall feel much better and freer.

Prior went up in smoke this morning over his mission being disbanded without his knowledge or consent, and yesterday Piave had a row with him over his imperious way of ordering everyone and everything to his exact particular liking. It is a great pity, because he has an ample brain, energy and determination but is utterly ruined by his senseless disgusting egoism which he signifies by the name of 'individualism'; the first trait he refuses to accept in any subordinate, English or Italian.

The Lysander was over this morning – God knows why – but did not descend. If it did it might not be able to take off again.

*17th November:* Another drop last night on Bakersfield, including 1 body for Rudolf and plenty of explosives for us. I was up until one in the morning writing a report of my visit to Gruppo Sud, and this proposed Training School. Tom has suddenly changed towards me and is being most pleasant – perhaps because he is at war with Mike and Piave.

Just before lunch Pat returned from his month's stay near Claut with the Ippolito Nievo. He has had an interesting time and quite a bit of fighting.

This afternoon we went down to the field but again Lizzie didn't turn up. Now it is not coming until the 24th. Have found a new HQ for our mission as the Divs. are returning to Ropa and it will be hell on earth and the tower of Babel combined. The Italians are a very gifted nation: they can do everything except fight and talk quietly.

*18th November* Moved to the new HQ this morning; a nice house that gets the sun all morning; however, I am keeping on my room in Tramonti for the time being. The Americans dropped 2 or 3 bombs this morning on our DZ, God bless 'em. Piave says the Garibaldini have had the British and Americans in a big way and want to shoot us all. Well, Well.

Grey, harshly grey, but streaked with silver, the mountains, cast their longer shadows every day. The little village half a kilometre from us will feel the sun's warmth no more until the beginning of March.

Every morning the earth and snow is frozen. This winter will be severe. Today the *19th* is Sunday, and the bells are heard in all the valley, very beautiful on the still air. We complete our second month here this evening. This morning we ate an English breakfast porridge and bacon which I myself cooked. It was delicious.

*Nov. 20th.* It is arranged that I go as 2nd in command to Paul [Brietsche] This morning we departed, of course after six km the car-broke down and we are spending this night at Poffabro within hailing distance of the Hun. All communist brethren around us, and no electric light. Tomorrow I hope to see John Ross, from whom a letter yesterday I received. Bless him.

*'Capt. J. Ross R.A. November 6th '44*
*Dear Richard,*

*Very glad to hear that you and your party are safe and sound. We heard today that your Major had gone back and may be returning but our informant was not quite definite.*

*All goes well with us but we have not had a single drop and never received our personal craft kit when we landed, so are in the same condition that-we arrived in!! However we live in hopes. We have moved around a lot but have only been chased once so far; the Major's ⁴ mountaineering skill helped us!*

*Paul B[reitsche] is with us and will stay here. When we have received our stuff we will go back to the other Division in our area. John O[rr]E[wing] is still with John Wilk.*

*You will be surprised to hear that I continue Bridge – the Div Commander is very keen!!*

*I hear you have a beard and presume it is an Imperial!! I had one for 10 days not by desire but*

174

*by necessity and did not like it.*

Tom is retired to bed after much wine and little to eat. I follow soon. After more wine.

Today is St. Cecilia's Day – *Nov. 22nd.* Yesterday at the hour of six we arose and continued our journey to Barcis. Tom went on ahead, I following with the baggage. We topped the pass in good time, tho' there was plenty of snow, and arrived at Andreis only half an hour after Tom and Franco. The snow is plenty and frozen in this valley. At two o'clock we heard Tilman had left yesterday, so I parted from Tom to continue my lone journey to Paul.

In Barcis, which is gutted by the Germans, I met Mario of the 5th Brigade who was ready to guide me on the first part of my journey. We arrived last night at a small house in the mountain hamlet of Pezzeda, an hour's march from Barcis. There we ate, and slept in a pleasant hay loft. This morning we have journied to Casa Columbera which is the local Battalion HQ; a difficult journey over frozen snow all the way. We are here at about 1300 metres. All the skis are out and ready for use. I stay here tonight and continue the march tomorrow. This morning the sky was a solid wall of blue but by 11o'clock so many bombers had passed over enemy- wards that we saw about five tenths cloud. At least 400 bombers must have been over from Italy this morning.

Ate at one pm, first food for 17 hours, but not really very hungry: afterwards made some tea with Grappa in it – excellent. I should not like to stay with this Battalion through the winter. Three small home made wooden huts on the side of a mountain – a very steep mountain too. Tilman is already a legend here. The night he stayed in Barcis he stripped and bathed in the Cellina Torrent; a cold night, and a swift and freezing stream. All the locals were very impressed.

*Nov. 27th* and now for five days I have not written. The night of St Cecilia we remembered in song, not of my choosing or singing, but of the Alpini. Words I knew not but the tunes were longing and sounds of the mountains, with here and there only a song of the Patriots interspersed. We slept four in a bunk close to, one of us being sick of a fever and crying continually in the night, so we burnt a light the darkness through and I could not sleep for a long time.

When day came coffee and Grappa and cheese, no washing and I and two companions started our ten hour march to Battalion Bixio. A hard march, there being snow all along and the paths frequently sheer over the plains four thousand feet below. We passed along the flanks of Monte Cavallo, the last great height before the plains and halted for a midday meal of salami and cheese, but it being cold we stayed not long and departed on frozen feet. We arrived with the Bixio at 6 o'clock, a journey of ten hours and a half. A good meal and more singing and a political discourse by Giorgio the commissario. This Battalion is now but fifteen strong, the promised rigours of winter and the last Rastrellamento having seduced the greater part, in fact of all these Brigades, to the softer delights of the plain and bondage. Next morning the *24th*, a short march to the next Battalion where I was held, having no pass, until Vittorio,[5] old friend at Maryland, came and vouched me safe and a friend.

And so eventually to Div HQ and a smiling Paul Brietsche to welcome me, Tilman and John Ross being on a visit to a neighbouring American. Paul was going well on Grappa, and I joined him in a beaker. Both their missions have had a heartbreaking time; chivvied from place to place by the Huns, no drops and are wearing the clothes they arrived in. When and if a drop arrives, Major Tilman and John are going to a new area west of the Piave and Paul and I will be in charge here. In this Veneto Group of Brigades there are only about 50 men, and the whole Div is about 100 strong.

*November 30th:* Life is as ever the same. We live here in squalid intimacy, sleeping shoulder to shoulder in long bunks. To wash we visit a frozen pond two hundred yards away – a cold and unsatisfactory business. Two women also inhabit here, and go down to the plains to buy necessaries. We patrol everyday, another cold business as my boots are letting in water. Today is St Andrew's Day, Thanksgiving Day in America and the P.M.'s 70th birthday. We have just heard that the three Americans sent on to Tramonti have returned, as a big Rastrellamento has started in Friuli, in fact they were shot up at 6 in the morning while with Frankio's Battalion, where they were staying the night. So none of our requests for Batteries etc will have got through. We were on the air for the first time in eighteen days the day before yesterday. The Commander sent us a 'pep' message, said he was sure Paul and I would work well together etc.

*Dec. 2nd.* Owing to the last 'rastrell' we have had to take a hand in reorganising the daily routines — all stand to at 6.30 in the morning, and patrols out from 5am to 2pm, by which time danger for the day is presumed over. Milo never got out of bed before 9.30 before, so this is an achievement. At 4.30 this afternoon joy of joys we received a positive crack for the new dropping ground; all activity, a cheerful supper and a large fill of Grappa and we trooped down, an hour's march to the DZ. Cold it was, but a clear and beautiful night, the full moon but two nights gone; the fires were fine, and all prepared, but by one am no plane and so home disconsolately, for a few hours rest, two unfortunates having to get up at 5 am for the first patrol.

*December 3rd.* Disquieting news this morning of a fascist-full truck which has offloaded in our area; we are packed up, Guards and patrols on all sides of the camp; at 11.15 another truck is arrived. Now sitting beside a fire that isn't there, I wait to go on patrol again, or flee into the woods. Very hungry. Terrific alarm at about 16.30 hours; we all pack up and go. Return for first meal for 25 hours at 19.30. Alarm subsided. After dinner down to Croccetto to collect batteries, food and wine, but enemy still there and unsafe to enter village. Return and sleep very well.

*December 9th.* Each day has been a repetition of the last. The forest smells of huns but so far they have not found our hide out. Patrols all day from 5.am until 2.pm, in which we all take our part. In fact guards are welcome burdens which carry a flask of Grappa with them.

*December 19th.* In the last ten days a lot has happened. We have had three big falls of snow. We have heard that the drop of Dec 2nd fell on the plains, and on the 13th Paul, Norman[6] and self moved to the Manin Battalion to await the next drop due since that date, but not yet arrived in spite of perfect nights occasionally. The Americans and New Zealander have returned as Tramonti is still being rastrelled, and no news of Tom, who was down with Malaria at the beginning of it. Another chap, Ashworth, South African fighter pilot who was shot down a week ago, has also joined us. If possible we are going to stay here in our own Malga after the drop, although Div HQ don't approve. Everyone is now lousy except myself, 'tho so far in small numbers only. Major Grumbles the American is an excellent fellow. We go to see him in Texas when war is finished.

Today is *Christmas Day.* What thoughts and contrasts. On the *22nd* the cold spell began. On an average since then it has been 15 degree below zero, and much more at night. We feel it owing to the fact that we are not properly equipped for winter here; the coldest part of Italy.

On the *23rd* Paul, Norman and the Major went down to the plains to try and fix up the Major's 109. Returning today, laden with bottles, we hear. Last night was a great feast with the Patriots and we were well and truly entertained by the Nievo Battalion. I sang 'Tit Willow' for them, introducing it as an English love song. As they didn't understand the words, it didn't matter. Afterwards we all gave them 'Tipperary' and other war songs, and they sang 'Di qui e di la' etc etc ad nauseam. Much wine and a good night's sleep. A Fascist prisoner was brought up last night. They are treating him quite well at present.

*Jan 6th 1945.* Twelfth Night – last day of Christmas. What a Christmas. On the day itself, they shot the Fascist after Christmas dinner. He was only 18 years old.

We made the most terrific cocktails out of rum, grappa and vermouth – terrific. By 9.pm only Paul and self were surviving. On Boxing Day nothing much. On *27th* two planes and Radio op., a Sgt, whiskey, food, clothes, arms and ammo. A terrific night. Titch got drunk, and the Major and John stayed up all night. Paul and I got to bed about 4.30 am and had four good hours. The next two days we divided and hid the spoils and prepared the Major and John and Victor for their departure which occurred on the night of the 30th after much jollification and speechifying. Dear John, I was sad to see him depart at the heels of the indomitable Major.

Great preparation for seeing in the New Year, and to another 2 plane drop. Using the Eureka one plane dropped right on the fires, but the other unloaded down on the plains, but all stuff recovered. We returned to the Malga for the New Year, all the stuff being secured by midnight. By God it was cold. Everyone drunk – we made tremendous speeches. Felt slightly well next morning.

John Ashworth and Grumbles having been fully kitted, departed for Tramonti on the 2nd. Very sorry to see John go, a 1st class chap. That evening our mail was found. Christmas mail for me from Mummy, Lalla, Aunts G & L, and a parcel from Mummy. Most cheering – several books including my dear 'Memoirs of a Fox Hunting Man', and the Nov Blackwood much appreciated by all.

Today is a beautifully warm sunshiny day – *Sunday 14th Jan*. It has snowed and been very cold since the 5th. So much snow has fallen that Mazari and I were unable to reach Nievo Battalion on the 7th.

On the *8th* I did manage to get down to Tigre's Battalion where I met two other POWS and saw the Yanks, Bob and Roland. They were happy; and decided to stay put for the winter. On the *11th* at approx 11.30 hrs we were surprised and attacked by 180 Germans with 4 mortars and HMG's.[7] We saved nothing except our skins and what we had on at the time. Only one of the HQ missing but he is believed safe.

Eventually at 18.30 we reached a small Malga overlooking Montaner, a small village. Next morning some food and Grappa arrived. Yesterday the 13th we decided to split up, and moved nearer Montaner and thank goodness some blankets arrived. Bill, Eddie and Nello [8] have gone to join Tigre for the time being, and Magro, Biondino, Cicco and Lola are leaving to prepare a place for us in the Alpago area. Now at least we have blankets, tobacco, Grappa and enough to eat.

No news from Paul; I have written twice since the catastrophe to tell him of our plight. Everyone thinks that we were very lucky to escape with our lives, and yesterday the Huns combed out Montaner, I suppose in the hope of finding some of the Partisans. The snow is really bad this year – coming sometimes up to our chests during the flight, and we may have to leave the mountains until March. It doesn't seem that we can do a great deal for the time being. However, we wait for Paul and the Div Commander to return.

*Jan 25th*. On the *19th* I left at 4.am with Joe, Mazari and Titch picking up Bill, Eddie and another of Tigre's on the way. By 09.30 we arrived at the Old barracks – burnt out but still standing. All our stuff was in it. Found the Radio Eureka and RBZ, petrol and oil. 4 and half hrs walk from there to DZ which used to take 40 mins.

We arrived at the DZ quite done in. The snow was frequently up to our chests, and we were all carrying at least 50lbs of kit. The Malga was empty, bare; nothing and no one visible. Got wood, a little straw from a nearby Malga, and proceeded to make a good fire and cook the one tin of sausages for our supper. It worked out about half a sausage per man, and this we enhanced with raw Marmalade which went down very well; then followed a great tea brewing orgy which lasted until half past eleven. By that time I was very tired, and sufficiently dry to go to bed, 'tho both blankets were still sopping. It was horribly cold but managed to sleep.

At 4. am Mazari and the animal man set off for the old Manin HQ to see if the Brigade were there at all. They arrived back at about 8.30; no one there, except 2 men who told us where Chirurgo had moved to approximately. I arranged that after breakfast (1 tin of bacon, powdered eggs, tea) they should go off, find Chirurgo, tell him we were expecting a drop that night, and send men to help carry the radio equipment.

Eventually the men arrived to help us at 2.pm and we were with Chirurgo at 3, where we had a very grateful dinner and glass of wine. The next thing was to see if we had a positive or negative; they were not too keen on having the drop, as the snow was so deep, and a rastrell was promised to arrive between the 17th and 20th, and this was the 20th.

At 4.30 we listened and out came the positive. I decided to have the drop near the present occupied Malgas as it was too far to the old DZ and anyway I trusted the RAF would not notice the small difference 'tho in fact we were 150 metres lower. "No wood" says Chirurgo; petrol torches suggests Lorenzo; excellent says I. No signalling gear says Joe, so Bianco rigs up a home made affair with a lid for the Morse signalling. We were all ready at eight, and the plane arrived at nine, and made many gyrations, but dropped everything at one go. One package of mills bombs exploded, having left its parachute behind. No one hurt.

All landed about 500 yards from the lights. I went to bed and next morning we received our wireless kit – and most wonderful our mail. No sign of the cigarettes, 'tho from odd English packets lying about it was obvious they had been found and opened. Mail: Two letters from Mummy, one from David, written in Holland, one from Dr Sims, and parcel from Kit containing Tovey on Beethoven's music and five Lit. Supplements – delicious. I am having some of the articles translated into Italian for the political benefit of these patriots e.g. the review of Mr Sumner Welles book on Europe.

We spent all day hiding kit in holes, and missed the messages at 4.30, and I was astounded when we got another positive at 6.30. The plane arrived at about 10 past 9 and made an excellent drop. Everything in it for the Partizan.

On the 22nd I decided that Joe should return to get the Radio cracking and Mazari, Bill, Eddie, Nello etc go with him as there was quite a lot of kit to carry. I would stay on one more night and go back next day if there was no drop. There wasn't.

A digression. Just found a verse I wrote be-fore the 'Rastrell' that really seems quite appropriate, as I was the first to be seen and shot at on top of the hill.

*February 4th.* Many vexatious days have passed, and the news is steadily better. We have moved 4 times in this region and are now right on the edge of the Mountain overlooking Montenar. This means alarms at all times, and today 9 huns came halfway up and then returned. Have made contact twice, but the bastards at base just wont receive or send messages. One Positive on the 30th but weather bad, and no plane. Paul writes they have had 5 Positives for M & J and only one drop.

We are now living better, getting about 3 eggs a day, and also plenty of wine. Grappa very scarce.

The plains are bombarded all day most days: Today it is simply terrific. Jerry is on the move, and 40,000 German troops have crossed the Piave Udinewards in the last 10 days. The weather is curious, yesterday snow, today very hot and like spring. We have it on good authority that there may be more snow but it will not get any colder. The radio is carefully hidden in a Malga about a kilometre away, whither goes Joe, Nello, and sometimes myself every day.

Yesterday we heard of the death of Gemma, one of our girls. She was shot by a German sentry on failing to stop when being challenged. RIP.

Shots being fired about 800 yards away: Cicco is just going off to have a look see. Possibly in Montaner itself, 'tho they said nearer.

This is the end of the diary. Although the war in Europe did not end until May 8th, in effect it was over in Italy at the end of April. Many of the German occupying forces surrendered to Italian Partisans, which was a great tribute to their courage and perseverance.

Richard flew south to Sienna in a very crowded Lysander with Paul Brietsche and Norman Norton on April 20th. There are a few letters which describe the euphoria of the time, in the interlude which follows the Partisan Poems. There is no doubt that Richard developed his great love of Italy and the Italian people during those months of 1944 – 45. The courage of the Partisans, and of the people in the villages who sheltered them was incredible, and beyond praise. If they were caught, they faced a certain and gruesome death.

## PARTISAN POEMS

### NO SOUND

One afternoon, we crept into a town
In trepidation; fearful that all life
Was not extinct; that the aloof
Blind walls were sensing the abrupt return
Of those whom we destroyed.
Slowly we gained the slope.
Curious and ungainly our approach
Like crabs, all scuttlewise, askew,
with sidelong glances. Sleep
was sovereign here; our weapons might not cowe
Such grotesque silence. Once

We knew these people, poor but satisfied
In living; now, lost in a senseless feud,
Their township tumbled by some ponderous lance
And they bereft, betrayed.
There was no sound, no life no movement, death
Reached out his everyday impersonal hand.
And now there lies another man beneath
The hill of Holy Cross; he was my friend.

## ODE TO A DEMIJOHN

O Golden Demijohn:
Sweet fitful promiser of joys undreamed,
Jealous provider of a wine, unnamed,
But peacefully slept upon.

Many the wines I've seen
Poured from your generous throat in simple song,
Black wine and silver, gentle wine and strong;
Even you've stomached fine

Champagne, the local mark,
Grappa so called, that makes the guardian hour
Dissolve in phantasie; or does a power
Of good, when in the dark

I wake and take my post,
And shiver out the early winter dawn:
You are the spirit, I am but a pawn,
A ghost.

And now your bowl is filled
Another day is cast, and we can say,
Better than by a clock, the time of day,
As you are killed.

'Tho one may come in stealth
With cup unlicensed steadied to your run
Frown not nor look too sourly on him;
He drinks it for his health

Perhaps. And you can spare
A little of your liquid gold for man
Who weary toils, but finds within the can
Surcease from Care.

## PIZZOC

On Pizzoc a cross is set
Looking away from Millifret
From whence, across the lake of death
Is Vicentin, two hundred metres more
Wreathed with God's breath.
And looking down one day I saw
The lake of Holy Cross below
Still frozen by the winds that blow
Across the Alps by winter's law
And no man moved beneath.

No man moves along the road
None tarry now beside the lake
Death stalks abroad

And upon this high hill
We free men bear the load PIZZOC
Of Italy; we die or kill
Gladly for her sake.
Down our men go
Four thousand feet or more below,
Destroy the road and rail,
Kill the unwary, slow
German. They never fail
To bring some casque a German wore,
A picture of some German whore,
That, gentlemen, is war.
Mercy, there is none
Expected from, or given to the hun.

[This poem, and Ode to a Demijohn, were kept with
the wartime diary]

TWO PATRIOTS

Raymond Lefevre, Frenchman.

Weep for a patriot – a Frenchman
Who died on this far side of the high mountains.
Who fought for his country and Italy
– Whose faith could not move mountains.

He gave his aid
To those who were afraid
And his love
He cast down as a glove

Defiant in the face
Of barbarian disgrace.

Yet he had little hope –
Just enough to cope.
With torture and the rope.

When he was hanged
The whole world stood arraigned
Pray that his soul
Escaped him whole.

## 2. THE PATRIOT

Beneath the shady Ides of March
Giuseppe moved. He was not good
For very much, but understood
Parched flesh and urgent heed of blood.

Cold knife which held the stare of death:
The cutting blade which sharpened life
To a still point of truth – while grief
Consumed his spirit underneath.

These esoteric facts he knew,
The mysteries of blood were hid.
But, in his dying, what he did
Was all the future bade him do.

## THE VENETO

The valiant plain
Is filled with an ancient peace
The quiet of compline,
And the silence of space.

An edge of night
Is thrusting back the day;
Little towns lie neat
As if laid out, to die.

A strange pity is here
Made manifest –
Pity is for hire –
But the age moves too fast.

Compassion eternal
For the children of men;
And the mountains kneel
In prayer, and remain

Watchful, The night passes
And peace comes with the morning:
The earth reposes,
Only the memory of grief remaining.

## VECCHIO

There was a rage.  I can remember
Anger seeping out from a twilight room.
It was a tired evening in December
Which sent a friend to his doom.

There was a meeting.  I do not know
The Whys and Wherefores bandied about,
But the sentence was final : He must go
Before the night was out.

There was a shot.  It shattered love
The only reason we had at all.
God – it seemed – and Satan were hand in glove
And great indeed the fall

Of one of them; I'm not sure which one
- It doesn't matter – a priest might know.
Henceforth the fight would be fought alone
With our conscience, red – as snow.


## CANZONE DA PARTIGIANI

The Mountains:   We are cold and silent now,
                 And the beech trees are bare.
                 The cattle have left their byre,
                 Quietly falls the snow.
                 We will sleep 'neath winters white
                 Covering, till the spell

Of spring is laid, and the pale
Wild flowers begin to show,

The Patriots:        It is for you we fight;
You are the land we love,
In winter or when the leaves
Put forth: In sun or sleet.
Our fortress during the night,
Our courage and our desire
You give us hope to soar
And triumph in defeat.

The Mountains:     Sing us your songs. O men,
Of the mountains – round your fire-
Say, are we harsh or fair,
Say will ye yet remain
When all Italy is yours
And peace is come again?
Though ye go, ye are not gone;
Your memory inherits the years.

# 13

## Interlude

April 27th 1945
[Italy]

Delightfull to be able to write again myself after so many days. I have forgotten how to write a letter so this will be more like a public notice than a conversation on paper – however?! I arrived back at base on the night 25th/26th and we were met at the drome by a chap whom we all knew very well before we went away and he very thoughtfully produced a bottle of Scotch which we drank neat. Yesterday we spent being interviewed, trying to get kit, lunching with the big noise, failing to get kit, meeting old friends and new enemies, shooting lines, comparing notes, wishing we'd decided to stay in 'till the end of the war – in fact not a dull or spare moment.

We had a small celebration last night – beginning sedately with dinner and the local champagne, the tempo gradually increased, and by the time we'd been thrown out of about six Yankee Messes, and taken a few American Colonels back to ours, it was a pretty hot show.

I was glad to find a few letters when I returned, as I had not received any since February. I received five batches during the seven months, and so I haven't received quite a few you wrote, but even so I was a lot luckier than many chaps on the job. So glad to hear David got home sound in wind and limb and enjoyed his leave. He must realise that literally I was unable to send letters – the cable I sent you in February was sent by radio. Anyway its lovely to be civilized once more, and leave is in the air.

Feeling very well. Hope the war over in a few days.

PS This letter is merely introductory – will write again very soon, and also to everyone in the next few days. Have talked to Nora[1] who was writing to you on my behalf – and thanked her muchly.

May 3rd 1945
[Italy]

Yesterday for the first time I visited Florence, the great city – and saw Giotto's tower and the Duomo, incredible exterior but miserable within – and Lorenzo's Palazzo and memories flooded me of Landor and Swinburne, the oldest and the youngest – the Brownings, and the English tradition in the flower city. We heard Rigoletto at teatro Verdi which was well performed and I enjoyed it.

The war for us is over in Italy – but no celebrations – One moment we were at war – having a drink in the bar, then peace descended – and we were still behaving like rational human beings . That night I went to a dance.

You will have a phone call shortly from Oliver Churchill, a Major, and the most charming fellow; you would like to meet him. He will probably be in London so invite yourself out to lunch with him. He will give you my news.

There is so much to write about and no permissible way of writing it, so for real news you must wait until I return. The weather has been vile lately, better today.  No more.  Love to Lalla – with love from Richard


May 7<sup>th</sup> 1945
[Italy]


Thank you for yours, and very glad to know you got my first one;  I am hanging about now doing nothing except reading, writing, and riding – We 'ave three 'osses 'ere.

I pray you call on one Canon Kettlewell, who lives in, and is rector of, Aylesbury.  He is a relation of a chap called Norman Norton – an escaped POW whom we picked up and used as an interpreter for eight months.  He is the most charming fellow and a very great friend of mine.  Norman says that the Canon has "two lovely daughters, and he also drinks and swears."  He sounds a good type, and I should like to meet him when I return.  Have you heard from Oliver yet I wonder?

I tried to sunbathe this afternoon, but it was so hot that I was constrained to retire to the splendid dimness of this delightful villa, to which we moved today.  Just before tea I had my first hot bath since September last year – I mean a real normal sort of bath, with delicate perfumes in the water – an Italian to scrub my back, and a chiropodist to cut my toenails.

I stayed with some Yanks the other day, and we did not bed down until 5 in the morning – frightfully gay but definitely wearing!

No more news – I am reading Proust – Delightful.

May 12ᵗʰ 1945

Many thanks for yours of the 5ᵗʰ. I delayed answering a day in case any news of my future movements came through. Needless to say, they haven't – but without wishing to raise your hopes too high, it is just possible I may get home this summer. I hope so. In the meantime we are so comfortable here that I feel it unnecessary to go gallivanting off on leave to some Italian city like Rome or Naples. We live in a fine villa – four Officers, with a staff of twelve to look after us, and several civilians – a cook and a laundress. We have three horses in the stables, and I ride before breakfast as it gets so hot later in the day.

At present we are in the middle of the asparagus and strawberry season, what a blest country where they come at the same time – wish I could send some home. I am being frightfully lazy and really enjoying it – gave a dinner party the other night, invited Jon Goody of the Regiment and two Americans – it was very successful, at least it lasted until 3am in the morning.

I received three Blackwoods while I was in the field, quite a few letters, 'tho not nearly all that you wrote, a Christmas parcel with lots of lovely odds and ends – which were all captured a week later – but no tobacco, perhaps it is not yet arrived. I am smoking not very much at present, three or four pipes a day and perhaps a couple of cigarettes, but am drinking a fair amount of the local wines – very health giving, I believe.

May 21st 1945
[Italy]

It has been arranged, and I am in the process of returning home for a month's leave – a month – mark you – which will be most delightful. Please do not write any more, as I have left the above address and letters will never catch me. We are so elusive, going the longest and most obscure way about everything.

I attended a wedding the other day. One of our fellows to a FANY, both of whom I know and like very much.

Do hope David won't have to occupy Germany. So boring!?

Can give you no dates, but hope to celebrate Waterloo chez nous.


**WAR LEAVE**


This was the magic of a month at home:
The train which left the station sharp on time,
Puffing contentedly through the still, green,
Countryside which Englishmen esteem.
No flattery that other lands assume,
No sudden picturesqueness, but the same
Awareness of the dignity of earth.
The living trees, the gaunt and gracious elms
Set in uprighteousness against a sky,
Echoing the varied pattern of the land
Unceasingly.

# 14

## Eastwards to Victory

On May 8th 1945 the war in Europe ended, but the war in the Far East against Japan continued. This war had started on December 7th 1941 when a large part of the American fleet was attacked at Pearl Harbour, their base in Hawaii. Japan went on to conquer many Pacific islands and territories. Hong Kong fell on Christmas day, and by February 15th 1942 both Rangoon and Singapore were in Japanese hands. Re-capturing these far-flung lands was a long job, and although by July 1945 much progress had been made, the war was by no means over.

Richard had some war leave at home, before flying to the Far East to continue SOE operations there. He landed at Karachi, where he spent some time in hospital recovering from Malaria. From there he went on to Ceylon, as it was then called, and waited for orders to be parachuted in to the Celebes (now Sulawesi) or some other occupied territory.

The Royal Sussex Regiment
Force 136, SEAC
[Karachi]

July 16th 1945

Just a line from Karachi where we arrived yesterday evening, and where I am spending a few days in hospital with malaria. Already I feel quite fit but they won't let me travel to Colombo for about a week I think.

We left from a station in Wiltshire on Saturday morning, lovely weather all the way, arriving at Malta at half past two for a late lunch. We got to Cairo about ten that night, had supper, and off again soon after midnight, for Shaiba, at the head of the Persian gulf; where we arrived about seven o'clock on Sunday morning.

We had breakfast there, a horribly hot place, and left about quarter past nine. It was soon after this that I had an attack of malaria, having felt very fit all the way. There was an RAF doctor, a Wing Commander , on board and he made me go sick at Karachi otherwise I should have gone on to Columbo this morning, however I expect it was wiser not to, and I shan't be long delayed – I hope.

As you can see it was a pretty swift journey; very comfortable and only twelve passengers on board. It's not too hot here in Karachi, but inclined to be sticky. It is a dull day and windy. I drove through the city last night and immediately remembered the peculiar smell of an Indian city – so different from the Arab cities – and much nicer. I really don't feel at all ill now, but the rest will do me good; I don't want to arrive at HQ completely washed up (or out).

Ain't it incredible; England on Saturday, India on Sunday. Heaven preserve us from the next war!

July 28th 1945
[Karachi]


Now at a convalescent home convalescing. A religious house, originally standing on a promontory outloooking the sea. A Sister Theresa appears to be in charge, a Holy Roman and a very nice woman.

The election results have reached here . I find them gratifying – I really think it is the best, 'tho I'm sorry for the slight on Mr Churchill;  he will regard it as one I'm afraid, and also sorry that Bevin is Foreign Secretary, 'tho it might have been Morrison, and that would have been worse. Sir Stanley prevailed, I see, the old humbug. I wonder how much Birkenhead did get over the Bhopal show?

I hope to be on my way to Ceylon any time after 2nd August. Have met two of our chaps in Karachi, one on the way to Australia, and the other to Ceylon. I am dining with him tonight in Karachi; we may go on together.

I don't like Karachi very much, it is a dull spot – nothing like Madras.  There is a wind and grey skies 'tho not much rain.  We can't bathe at this season of the year owing to innumerable stinging jelly fish which frequent these waters.  Not nearly so much fun as in Italy – what perfection in retrospect.

I wish I was at home again, but really thought I could just about "make" Ceylon. Anyway I should be cured, I'm as yellow as a Chinaman, the cure, they say, little yellow pills, not quinine.

Have you seen or heard from the Thompsons at all- how's Palmer. [1] I'm still working on the play – difficult.

I expect David will be on leave by the time this arrives.

August 6th 1945
[Ceylon]

Well, I left the Convalescent home on August 2nd and on the third at mid day embarked on the last stage of the journey by Tata air line – It is an all

Indian Civil aviation company, and a very good one too. We stayed the night in Bombay, 'tho not in the town, and next morning we had two breakfasts, one at a twilight hour in Bombay, and the other at a respectable 10 o'clock in Hyderabad; and so we pressed on to keep a luncheon engagement in Madras – very good curry with pompadours and a view of the Adyar Club from the air. We flew straight down the coast and had tea in Columbo.

Here I find no-one I know, but have made a couple of acquaintances. Am settling in, but the future is vague. Today is Sunday, and all very peaceful. The climate seems good, and we live in curious wicker huts. The camp is well shaded by palm trees and one goes about in danger of a coconut falling nastily on ones head.

I haven't lost the little pen, but having had to empty it because of air pressure in the plane, have not yet bothered to fill it again – besides, I like a pencil much better – pens are messy affairs and remind me of examinations.

I'm sorry about poor old Bertram,[2] he's a gay old spark, and I suppose he regards crossing the road as an adventure, 'tho I think at his age his girl friends should come and see him.

Dies Irae MCMXLV [postmarked August 18th]
[Ceylon]

I expect too that you are writing to me today. We heard the news this morning. Thank God it has come at last; it will mean a lot that David will not be coming out here; a great load off your mind.

We don't yet know what we will be doing, but it seems most probable that a use will be found for us, probably further East; it should not be a long job though, and I don't intend staying out here doing an occupation job; but would like to see Japan. I was all set up and prepared for an operation; but things will be different now. No more parachuting I hope.

We are very quiet today – a holiday, but I didn't feel like beating up Colombo. I'm so glad the war is finished (apart from Spain!)

There is no news this is just a Victory Valentine.

On August 6th the atomic bomb was dropped on Hiroshima, and two days later another was dropped on Nagasaki. The Japanese finally surrendered on August 15th. Richard remained in Ceylon. I think he might still have been sent to one of the Dutch East Indian Islands, for not all the Japanese surrendered immediately, and it is clear from the following letters that some further action was possible.

VICTORY

Is victory proclaimed in an outstanding phrase,
Or sculp'd and chisell'd, as a Phidian frieze?
Should we chant it as a chorus or an ode
Or suffer our dead heroes to be deified?
Let undertakers now construct a bier
Unparalleled for boys, whose mothers bore
The pain of life and death and hopelessness.


But victory is not concerned with dying
Or the dead – but with the living, the doing;

So think of them sadly, perhaps, but give your mind
To noble possibilities of remake and mend.
We share old memories with death; and you
And all mankind remembering, answer 'yea,
Forward' – with pain, but without hopelessness.


August 22nd 1945

Yours of August 12 arrived two days ago and Lalla's letter with Beechcomber, for both of which many thanks. I think it were better if you keep the book, which sounds very interesting, at home, as everything is still so unsettled. I have no more idea of our eventual fate than has the man in the moon – or the local big noises.

In Madras we had only a very swift lunch at the airport – which is not far from the Adyer Club – we had a good view of it from the air. I must go there on leave. There is absolutely no news except that Paul Brietsche arrived here last night, very fit and full of beans, and also engaged again. I was most pleased to see him, he said he rang you up on leave, about a day after I left – most annoying.

On Sunday I attended a cricket match as third reserve – luckily my services were not required, but it was a pleasant day, and the club was very nice – out in the country.

By the way I wrote to Holts asking them to credit the Imperial Bank with £100, as I may go a long time without pay being credited out here. So don't get alarmed when the next balance comes in!

August [24th?] 1945 [Colombo]

No letters lately arrived, but everyone appears to be in the same boat, so I imagine the hold up is due to transportation.

Life is excessively boring here. Last week I journeyed to Kandy – did I tell you – with Paul Brietsche. A very lovely place, a fine setting for the jewel that is the temple, buddhist, and contains the Buddha's tooth. I have been twice to the cinema lately, nothing to do else, saw " For Whom the Bell Tolls", which I liked, reservedly, for the occasional scenes which were echoes of our own mountain life in the Dolomites – Just little things, like scooping the wine out of a large, and doubtless dirty, metal basin; and the ambush was well done too. But they missed the whole political point, and substituted vapid and extraordinarily unintelligent love scenes – piffle! Though Ingrid Bergman is very beautiful, I think.

The other was "Song of Bernadette" which I think was magnificent, especially the girl and the falcon faced sister who only believed when it was too late. Startlingly good propaganda for the Romish church, I wonder if that *is* the idea.

I am now weekending in Colombo writing a bit – reading a bit. If you get a chance try and read some of Graham Greene's books; the three best, I think, are "England Made Me", "The Power and the Glory", and "Brighton Rock" and are excellent. You remember we saw the play in London three years ago.

I am really staying here because of two friends who are in hospital; and they get fed up and lonely, and need someone to arrange things for them. I've been to see a Dutch doctor, a charming fellow, on behalf of one of them; but the authorities were so upset and "hurt", that we had to give up the idea of letting Richard be treated by him. Richard Lea is one of our chaps out here, a great friend of Paul's, and more recently, of mine.

I think I've already got a library of about 30 books. God knows what I should do with them when I come home, if I come by air, but that don't seem very likely yet, it is all very slow.

Is David likely to get out soon? I hope so.

Royal Sussex Regiment   [Colombo]
ME25 Force 136  SEAC

August 30th 1945

I had hoped that by now I would have heard definitely of future plans as regards being used for any purpose out here, but we are still vague, 'tho I am officially at 24 hours notice to drop in anywhere. We are staying chiefly in Colombo itself as the camp is 25 miles out – I am now bathing a lot and becoming very brown. Paul, John Ferrer and I gang about most of the time together. Paul is again engaged to be married – in England, and is anxious to get home again. He has offered me a job in his firm after the war, wholesale importing with much jaunting about the Continent – Italy for Venetian glass etc. Thus I shall be able to write and yet be assured of something to live on! Do you like the idea – if it comes off? Of course I shan't say anything about leaving the army yet – I may have to stay another two years.

We are going "up country" on Saturday to Nogombo – a lovely name – to bathe and eat shell fish and then coming back to the Hotel for the official Victory Ball. Luckily we missed the Victory Parade, but the local municipal Council is furious because they were not given better seats, or accorded proper respect or some such tommy rot.

As a matter of fact this island stinks – the Black Market rampant in everything, and complete apathy towards the war shown by all. I 'ates it and am determined to winter in Cairo if I can't get home.

I am really feeling much fitter now – hope I've seen the last of the malaria. I hope you are all bearing up under the rigours of an English Summer – and the menagerie all in fine fettle.

September 1945[7th][Colombo]

Alarms and excursions and whatnots – have been quite unable to write for the last few days, as we were all set for doings of a kind that you may imagine; we chased all over the island, then it was cancelled, then I was on something else, and now we are going back again to the camp.

You can imagine I am disgruntled – but I hope before long to be visiting  the place where grandfather spent his early years, and I believe Richard Henry lived for a long time! Am also very busy learning Malayan, and doing a spot of typewriting. This is late at night – at least it seemeth late; but I'm quite weary, which is really the matter.

In a way there is a great sufficiency of interest here. We have in our Mess every nationality under the sun – American, Canadian, Dutch, Belgian, French, Spanish, most of the Eastern races – it is really very fascinating; funnily enough, no Italians!

Well, it is morning now. I finish this letter because we begin an early day. This is the best part of it, cool and yet no wind, and no glaring sun. I have just had some pau pau – wery nice. There is no news, but tomorrow I hope to write a really long letter about nothing at all.

September 1945    [Colombo]

I give thanks, Madam, for your letters dated 21, 23, and 26 July, which, having wandered wearily, have at last found refuge here; these were they which missed me at the beginning of my travelling – Karachi, I suppose, and as I was not down here, they've been sent to each camp in turn . Even more welcome is yours of 8th September.

I am learning Malayan, an easy, colloquial language, but I have no tongue I'm afraid, or else I love my own language too much. I am getting very brown, sea bathing every day, absolutely marvellous. My new camp is right on the sea, and not far from Colombo.

If I am unable to write in the near future, instead of letters, you will be getting a fortnightly cable, so don't worry when the first is delivered – but I shall certainly be writing again before that. Nothing is settled and we live from day to day.

Last night we threw a big dance at the Grand Oriental hotel; it was, I think, a big success, and luckily ended at midnight prompt. Paul and John Farrer are still kicking their heels, but hope to go home shortly. They've both done five years abroad.

A.D. xij kal Nov MCMXLV
Trafalgar Day 1945 [October 21st] [Colombo]

Many greetings this day, which we have celebrated with Beethoven's 5th, Gracie Fields singing Ave Maria, and a curious South African interlude. Nelson's blood was not available. "Nelson confides", "England expects", and I look very fit in the mirror in front of me now.

We have moved again. The rains have been tremendous and there is no more sea. I have just recovered from a poisoned foot – painful, but nothing more. Tonight is the full moon, and the palm trees look like windmills across the sky – big palm fronds clutching at the moon.

There is no news – absolutely nothing. More waiting about even, than in the war. It is difficult to imagine we are at peace. In the meantime my chess is improving as I play usually two games a day.

October 28th 1945 [Colombo]

I hope this reaches you exactly on the fourth, to wish you many, many, Happy returns of the day. I do wish I was at home for your birthday and Christmas, it is a long time now since I was, but I hope you have a very happy one, and good weather after the terrible gale which we read about in the local papers. Thank you very much for the Emlyn Williams play which arrived yesterday, I have begun reading it, and like it very much. I look forward to the arrival of the Dante very much. Reading matter is a little scarce unless you are in Colombo or Kandy. It is probable that I shall be changing jobs very shortly; things seem to have reached an impasse in our section, and I shall probably jump at a chance which has been offered, but more of that when I know for certain.

We went down to Galle the other day, a very delightful old place, with a Portuguese fort. Very quiet, peaceful, and rather like an Italian town. I got your birthday present there – I hope you will like some silk stockings – which I hope to send off shortly with some tea, unless one of our chaps goes back by boat.

As for me I wish I'd never come out here – 'tho it's true if I hadn't got malaria at Karachi I should have been in the field within a fortnight. Administration and direction leaves a lot to be desired when compared with the European war – however...! I shall hold a birthday party for you on the 4th.

# 15

## Bangkok

Fortunately, instead of dropping in to the Celebes, or other Dutch East Indian islands, Richard went to Bangkok, unlikely as it may seem, as part of a team to pursue Psychological Warfare. There are very few letters from now on which have been kept, although he still wrote regularly, but Richard was also busy writing poetry.

Royal Sussex Regiment   [Bangkok]
c/o GS(I)  Branch
Main HQ 7<sup>th</sup> Indian Div  SEAC
November 11<sup>th</sup> 1945

What a long address; and all it really means is that I am now in Bangkok.  I left Kandy on Monday morning, and arriving in Colombo found Paul Brietsche and John Farrer,  Paul still waiting to go home.  He missed a plane the week before, and it crashed in Malta; all hands lost.  So he was well out of that.  Then I left Colombo at about midnight, flew all night and came down at Pegu, near Rangoon, only twenty minutes away. I was kept hanging about the airport some time and then sent off to a reception camp, as there was no plane going to Bangkok until Thursday. The camp was an appalling place, not even a mosquito net; however I wandered round the town and saw the famous Shive Dragon Pagoda.

Rangoon had been pretty severely bombed but things are settling down again now.  On Thursday morning early we left and arrived at Bangkok about

10:30 in the morning. It is only two and a half hours flying time.

Bangkok is a very fine city, and has not been much affected by the war. I am living in a big hotel in the main street; it is still run by the civilian owners. I am working, too, with a civilian, Mr Bullock, who knows Thailand very well and talks like a native. At the minute we are experiencing considerable opposition from military sources, but I hope it will all soon be settled on a higher level. There are thousands of Japs here working on odd jobs; all very smarmy and subservient, and saluting right, left and centre. I haven't done any sightseeing yet, but hope to before long.

There has been no mail arrived for me yet, but I hope it will catch up soon. Let me know how long this takes to get back. I must stop now as the mail is just about to go, and I can't post this at the hotel.

PW Mission
ALF (SIAM)

New Years Day '46

I expect you are writing today, and so I do, to wish again a most hopeful New Year, which has begun auspiciously out here with the promulgation of the Treaty between Great Britain and India on the one hand, and Siam on t'other. Every building in all roads is flying the Thai and / or Chinese flags, and all the Government buildings fly the Jack, the Tricoleur, the Thai flag, the Chinese, and the Soviet banner. Most of the Jacks are hoisted upside down! with typical efficiency. The weather is very nice now, cold enough for a blanket at night, but not too cold for a cold bath morning and evening.

I feel sorry for David; they seem to be getting rotten weather this year. When I was there it was the best winter for years, and we got no real rain until the middle of January, and it was all over by the end of February. I know it can be miserable, and very cold.

I'm afraid the poem will have to wait, as 'tho I've written several things, none come up to even my standard – and it must be good. In part this is due to the large number of books which I am reading at the present. I'm really getting my Italian history at my fingertips. Wish I'd known as much about the various Garibaldini then as I do now.

There is really no news. I had a quiet New Year, cutting a dance and was asleep long before the passing. It seemed silly to ring out with so much joy a Year, such as we have not known for centuries, and give such a welcome to a, well, highly problematical future. I've finished the delightful book Virgil to M but will always read it again with great pleasure especially the 'Virgil' and 'Tasso' chapters.

F.E.P. Detachment
B.T. (SIAM)

Feb 20<sup>th</sup> '46

The postman, after an uneasy sleep, seems to be awakening. Yours of the 11<sup>th</sup> arrived today, 9 days – not bad at all. Life here is quiet but very busy – we continually enlarge our scope. And for the most part I am getting the evenings to myself to read, or try to write. Tomorrow however we are giving a small dinner party to Editors etc., men on local papers. The way to their hearts we hope is through their tummies – pretty massive ones too. I hope its a success. The mango season is just begun, our first tomorrow.

We had some friends to dinner on Saturday, and then they took us to hear the revived 'Fine Arts' orchestra. Mozart's 'Juppiter', Grieg's Piano Concerto, 'Oberon' overture, and 'Casse Noisette.' Not bad really, and afterwards we supped at a strange Chinese Restaurant down town. We also had a rather large fire in one portion of the town. A nasty business and a monument to the inefficiency of the town council. The first engine arrived an hour after the fire began, and then of course there was no water.

I'm glad Moore is settled. I'm not surprised about Paul marrying again; he said he was when we were in Colombo. Tell him to write; he owes me a letter. I feel most sorry for David, Palestine can be dreadful at this time of year especially under canvas. All the same I'd rather be there than here – a question of sympathies and other days I suppose.

The tobacco is'nt arrived yet but I have great hopes in the near future. I think I shall be leaving Bangkok about the beginning of April. Who knows – I may get straight home. India is not the sort of place I dream of. Full sovereignty I think in the next 4 or 5 months. What is Bevin playing at I wonder. And USSR, and USA. We're all in an applecart, going down hill – who's going to upset it?

Forward Base
Psychological Warfare Division
SEAC
[16th Nov '46]
I have put off and put off until I could tell you something definite, but even today (16th) there is no

211

definite news of which boat or when. The Otranto came in some time ago but has pushed on to Hong Kong. The Queen of B is now expected on the 19$^{th}$. So I will send you a wire the day before I sail, and hope that you can inform David in time for him to 'make' Port Said.

I'm afraid that several of your letters have been lost in the aircrash t'other day, at least I haven't had a letter for a fortnight now.

The trip to Sumatra had to be cancelled, which was most annoying, because Chris was going away 'up country' for a fortnight. However I have found a small island and hire a small motor boat and bathe and sunbathe most days.

It is pelting with rain now 10 o'clock, morning, and is so dark that I can scarcely see to write – lots of thunder and lightning. That one sounded like a 10,000 lb bomb going off; the storm is almost directly overhead, and some parts of Singapore flood after half an hours rain – its great fun.

Will you please take out a licence for my Browning automatic no 102981 as from this month, I think, because I don't want to be put in gaol for five years on arrival at Liverpool (I'm afraid) or Southampton (I hope). Well this will be the last letter before Colombo – where we are sure, I think, to stop. I should be in Merrie England for sure by the middle of November and only wish it could have been in time for your birthday. Don't forget Trafalgar and see you very soon.

# LAND OF THE PEACOCK THRONE

In this land
Of the peacock throne,
In this coloured island,
It is hard to remember
Autumn at home.
Mentem mortalia tangent;
But here is the earth immortal
And death such an every day affair.
I cannot think in terms of September
And the autumnal decay of the year.

At home is a drama of slow dying;
But, with surcease is sown another seed.
And each year renews this promise
And wakes in the spring.

Here there is neither awareness of life,
Nor realisation of death.
Only the blinding sun above aloof,
And the blind earth beneath.

## FRIEND

Are you in love with death, who would recall,
The flesh of those lost years?
They are the mourning headstones of our hopes
And hold a memory too close for tears.
Would you rebuild an image – in dull bricks?
There are too many corpses wasting now
By the green banks of Styx.
O think of me my friend, for in my head
One thought, one hopelessness, that you are dead.


## THE STOIC FARMER

"Il faut cultiver notre jardin"
That was the burden of war
Heard above the din of the sky devils,
And the rumour of evils under water,
And rumblings of tank tracks on tarmac,
Echoing from afar.


The old farmers who knew no French
Took up the lands burden.
No guerdon expected, they toiled
For earth and countries sake.
Their henchmen and women have felt
Sad at the setting down of harrow and rake.

Pray that above the more raucous din of peace,
"Il faut cultiver notre jardin"
Will find increase.

PEACE

Now the great battle of peace begins:
The giants have taken their cue and withdrawn
From the stage – cui bono- who gains
When the mighty voice is silent,
And we have lost
Our supply of spiritual benzedrine.


If we were drugged into winning
Can we be dragged with eyes open,
Through the blackmarket of peace, whining
For an opiate that will ease a nations pain.
We have no stomach for peace;
The pace is too hard, and the palm
Grease to the great; there are so many pies,
But others have taken the plums.


Victory has left us bereft
Of drugs, and illusion, and dope:
Then let us cling to the raft
Of reality, on this day of dupes.

# REMINISCENCE SWINGAPORE 1946

Caldicott
There was a green continual hush
About the house, and small boys ran about
On pitiless brown feet, and sang unreal songs
In a sad old tongue which knew its impotence;
And the green twilight lasted all the day.

Sundowners 6:30pm
Evening was cool, and seated by a window
We felt the last sun's cold absolving ray
Waiver a blessing; Then the peerless night
Turned a remotest green to grey
and darkness.

Goodness how sad
Angling in the lake of darkness
Old Emperors and Popes send forth a cry
– Stunning the trivial aeons with despair -
To pierce us when we are about to die.
Tears streaming down to millstones turned
Tears of a million million dead
Weeping away the living rock,
Sasso, on which a creed is set
On which they tried the paraclete.

Et mentem mortalia
Tangunt.
Our mortal death is no eirenicon –
Breath, hold a guarantee
Against despair so aweful, so profound
That Hell is a regretted levity.
The sum of all our sadness graves

Recondite nothings on each candid face
– But grieve for sorrows yet in store
And pray for us in our disgrace
By the dead sea shore.


## REVERIE ON CALDECOTT


Night is a time for crying
Then tears appear like stars.
The moon ascends the darkened stairs
While Judas is betraying
God.   And a cold wind stirs

The boughs of sleeping trees
Soon dead, and dead beside
The sevenfold town of Troy
Let fall another seed
Give earth another try.

Hoplites and hope are dreams
Achilles' heel is pierced
And silent chariots lumber past
The post in ruined hippodromes
To the beat of an unheard anapaest ...
The strivings of today
Will be legends tomorrow
And we are due to die
To thrill them to the marrow . . .

No matter what we do
We cannot know their sorrow.


## TURNING CLOCKWISE

The world was turning clockwise
When I sailed from Singapore
And wisdom was reflected
In the wisecrack of a whore.

We passed the Isles of Wisdom
And sailed the Seas of Peace
The mountains still looked down from Spain
Antolyans from Greece.

The world was green in spring-time,
But foggy in Soho
The master mariner was sick
And stayed the ebb and flow.

The King was counting concubines
And David got no heat
The maid was in a parlous state,
And Maida Vale was beat.

The housewives talking turkey
The soldiers talking shop
The MPs merely talking –
Cerberus with his sop

Proved that the world was laughing
At something up its sleeve
And I could not weep for laughing
And so I merely grieve.

# 16

## Malta and Trieste

Richard remained in the army until 1952. He continued to write home, at first from Malta, where he was glad to escape from the exceptional cold and bleak conditions of the 1946-47 winter, and later from Trieste. Malta was a British base in the Mediterranean, which had withstood appalling bombardment from German and Italian planes during WWII. As a result, King George VIth awarded the island the George Cross in April 1942, the highest civilian decoration. Richard is very conscious of this, heading each letter "Malta, G.C."

Toulon
21st Feb 47

Herewith the first of many, and many apologies for a not sooner intimation of my whereabouts. It was too sad, on arriving in Calais, to be rerouted to Malta G.C., where, I understand, I have a reasonable chance of meeting the 2nd Battalion. However, there it is; I am cheated of my Italian trip, condemned to the petty provincialism of Malta for three soul-ennervating years.

Luckily I met a rather pleasant fellow, I forget his name, and we have painted red the adjacent towns. We had the most appalling journey down here: snow and ice and no heating. We drank rum all through the night and were frozen stiff next morning somewhere near Dijon. I am doing all I can to help the 'Entente Cordiale' by saying what wonderful people the Italians are. Not very many Frenchmen seem to agree with me. The Mistral is blowing here and Spring seems too far away.

I can't say when I shall arrive in Malta but I think about the 1st of March; I will send my address by wire unless I can telephone you. I hope that winter has sprung no more cruel surprises.

Malta GC
2.iii.47

At last I can sit down – it being a Sunday – and write the sort of letter you said you would like. So rough, alas, was the Gulf of Lions and the seas surrounding Corsica and Sardinia that, creeping down their Western shores we were driven far south and sight Cape Bon earlier on Friday Morning. Thus it was impossible to reach Malta on Friday at all, and we had a 3rd night on the ghastly 'Empire Anvil'. I say 'we' because I was companioned by one Mathew Lees whom last I saw in Belfast in '39. He was down to Captain which made me forbode and mutter 'absit omen'. However all nightmares come to an end and we entered the Grand Harbour early on Saturday (yesterday) morning.

We are situate in the centre of the Island, and the view is superb. Being high up we get a delicious breeze and I look forth from a cloistered balcony over a gorge towards the ancient Saracenic city of M'dina with its superb and baroque Cathedral of St Paul. Its appearance is romantic in the extreme and the bells wake me up at 6 am. What more could be desired – as long as I must be in Malta at all. The island is very green just now and the temperature pleasant, rather like a fine June day in England. I think summer will be oppressive.

I have run into several old acquaintances and one old friend – Noel Ormerod. He is married and his wife is here. There are nearly 50 officers at present so there won't be much for me to do. I have arranged for Italian lessons and hope one day to take the army interpreters exam, thereby adding to my emoluments. Unfortunately we have too many Majors – 2 transferred from the 1st Battalion when it was known they were going to Palestine – and the Commander has told me that he is afraid etc etc etc. So I told him I couldn't care less, though of course I do. Do you think I should apply for the 1st? I think I could hold down my crown out there. Huxford the 2 i/c I used to know at the Depot, a nice quiet chap who was taken prisoner in '40 with the 2nd. Tomorrow we shall be told what we have to do. I may go on a course, I hope so.

Toulon was most unpleasant. We were there well over a week; I hope you got my last letter. A very badly run, wet, indifferent, and muddled camp. It is a very good thing that it is to be closed down this month. I don't think this Battalion enjoyed Italy very much. They speak not with enthusiasm.

It is now lunch and post time so I must end. Will write again when I know my fate.


Malta GC
March 11th 1947


Yours dated the 7th arrived here on the 9th which is not bad going. Thank you very much for it. Will you please send on all the mail if you are still keeping it. I confess I should like to see this certificate of service in Italy. Thank you very much for paying the hatter. I meant to go and see him when passing through London and as usual forgot all about him though I did go to Jones.

My last bag turned up safely 'tho someone, or something, had ripped off one of the zips. I am in command now of 'D' company, a cadre company, controlling weapons training and education, really not very much to do. Unfortunately the Battalion on Friday received an order to go into 'Suspended Animation' for 9 years and we are therefore going to disband. I can only wait and see what this will bring forth – sweetness of some sort, I sincerely hope. It is on the whole pleasant to rejoin the Battalion; I find I like them more than I thought I did.

We went and had a drink chez Noel Ormerod the other night; met his wife for the 1st time although she says we have met before. Yesterday I had to defend a man at a DCM – the charge was desertion. Noel was prosecuting, and it quite spoiled the week end as I had to go chasing evidence all round the Town. However I found time to go to a performance of Rigolleto at the Local Opera House. It was a very matey affair and although the singing don't last for 2 hours the performance lasted double that. The intervals were very long and everyone ate cheese sandwiches – 5d a time. I thoroughly enjoyed the opera which was old fashioned and heroic, with bouquets and things for the soprano. 'La Donne e mobile' didn't succeed but the quartet 'Bella figlia dell'amore' was terrific.

I do hope this predicted thaw is the real thing this time. It must have been absolutely awful these last few weeks – incredible for England, but perhaps you will be spared the March winds.

Malta GC
March 19th 47

Thank you very much – everything is now arrived, to wit...... the certificate which was gratifying, and a Bill from Jones – which wasn't. Thank you very much for the birthday present in advance, and I have already spent part of it in buying the Complete Work of William Blake published by the Nonsuch Library in One vol (about 900 pages) a very good edition indeed. The bookshops seem very good here in many ways 'tho there are curious omissions.

I am going to call on the Navy today – very peculiar hours, one goes between 1130 and 1300 hrs and drinks gin. In Malta no one calls in the afternoon. I am up to my eyes in work having been elected – or nominated – Secretary to the Malta Command Small Arms Meeting which takes place at the end of April. There is an enormous amount to be done and as I'm also on the Officers Mess Committee and we are giving a large Dance, I haven't much time.

Last Sunday I spent a pleasant afternoon on the beach on the N.W. side of the Island. I didn't bathe remembering how chilly it was at Haifa towards the end of April, but a lot of chaps did and very quickly came out protesting vigorously how warm and jolly it was.

Everyone is talking about the terrible, catastrophic weather in England. I do hope by now things are better 'tho the floods sound almost as bad as the snow. 'O wind, if winter comes can Spring be far behind' but is there even spring now before the wet and wintry summer sets in. I feel ashamed of coming to this mild island.

The GOC here was a Company Commander

at the RMC when I was there – Davidson, of No 4 Company. The Regiment seems to have made a good impression here. I have heard several civilians, myself in civilian clothes, compare them very favourably to our predecessors. The chap I defended was found Not Guilty of desertion but guilty of Absence. He got 84 days which was'nt too bad.

Malta GC

March, going out like a lamb

Many thanks for all the news and not too bad news; I'm very glad the weather is improving. I have had a busy time. On Wednesday I went to tea with the 'Times of Malta' and then on to a cocktail party. We were taken along by Mabel Strickland who is the owner and director of the paper and a very powerful woman on the island. It was somebody else's party – someone I've never met, but that didn't apparently matter, and I had a very jolly time.

Miss Strickland asked me to write two thousand word articles on Italy which I am going to do for the Times. I hope they'll accept it as worthy of their high (?) standard. I have also written a poem, and a highly astringent letter to an imaginary friend on the subject of life here generally and the disbandment of the Regiment in particular. I must say I did'nt think the Colonel would pass it as I had several pots at the War Office but he was highly amused and said 'I didn't know you had a *mind* like this.' What could he have meant, I wonder? The general betting is that the editor won't publish it.

I am planning to spend Easter on Gozo, the neighbouring island, with the second in command of the Battalion and my 2 subalterns. A nice weekend in the sun. I have put in to become an interpreter – very brave of me I consider, but a straw to clutch at Italiawards.

Everyone is accepting the invitation to a dance – from the Lt Governor downward. I insisted on asking the Archbishop of Malta (Sir Michael Gonzi) but he has refused and everybody is pleased – I don't know why. I believe he is very charming.


Malta GC.
13 April 47


We have had a very hectic week ending up with a gymkhana yesterday in which I was rash enough to ride. I went in for 2 races, one in which we had to dismount halfway, get an apple out of bucket of water by mouth, and then race back. The other was a business of knocking a polo ball through sticks and round sticks, a sort of equestrian croquet. I didn't originally go in for this but the Colonel had, and didn't want to ride himself, so I took his place. Anyway I managed to hit the ball, and as a result think I should take up Polo. It was really great fun, 'tho the first time I've ridden for three or four years.

Our dance on Tuesday was a terrific success. I believe it was agreed to be the best dance in Malta for years. Everyone came, except the Archbishop, and even the bigwigs stayed until long after midnight.

I am so pleased to hear that spring has really come to England. The latest news is that we are returning about the end of May to assist the new Territorial army in first training this summer. I don't know what will happen about my application, but the C.O has told me I am to take over command of Support Company when the rifle meeting is finished. I don't know anything about carriers or mortars but I suppose I shall learn. It will be nice to come back in the summer and I shall take my extra leave.

Nothing, however, is certain, and there are liable to be more changes. From now on I shall give up trying for different jobs and places, and just go whither I am bidden.

We have had no baths since I came back owing to the fuel shortage! Isn't it awful. The lack is world wide, and our lights have taken to going off suddenly in the evening.

[Malta]
24th April 1947

An awful short line in haste as we approach this wretched Rifle meeting date. Thankyou for yours of the 17th. I had a very quiet birthday but enjoyed it very much with one or two friends. Thank you also for the 'Voice of the World' which I find most interesting and a very good idea. I hope it does eventually produce in several languages.

At the Battalion Rifle meeting my Company (19 full strength) won one event and came second in two in the whole affair. Other companies (80-100) were very sour. I was Captain in the event we won; a strenuous affair running down the range. We also had the 3rd, 5th, 8th, 9th and 10th places in the individual championship. I was 9th. It was quite enjoyable and I now have a cigarette lighter which I shall undoubtedly lose.

5.v.47

[Malta]

Have just spent a weekend at Gozo recuperating (!) from the rifle meeting – which was quite successful. Today I take over command of 'Support' Company – an awful business! Thank you for your two letters and the enclosed from the Pay Office – which was notice of my war Gratuity, £145. Not bad!

I don't think its worth now sending 'Listeners' as we are due to leave at the end of the month. But I should like the Literary articles kept if possible. I think I can get some dungarees for David. And hope to bring back odds and ends in the food and commodity line – what do we need most?

By the way – tell me what you think of the lace. Is it genuine. I'm told so, but don't know.

If anyone wants a motor car I can order it here and it will be delivered in June in ENGLAND!! Of course I shall want a commission!

After Malta, Richard moved to Trieste via Udine where he was very happy to renew acquaintance with beloved Italy and his Italian friends. Trieste was seized by the Germans in 1943, but in 1945 the territory was occupied by Tito and claimed for Yugoslavia. This was regarded as a threat to the West. In 1947 it was divided. The southern part, which included the port, was placed under British-US military administration ; the northern part, where the city of Pola (more correctly Pula) was located, remained in Yugoslavia. Richard was part of the British force in 1947. It was in Trieste that he wrote the poem about the women of Pola. On leaving the city, when it became part of Yugoslavia, the Italians took even their dead with them. The first letter is written from Le Busette, the house belonging to Victor Gozzer, Richard's great friend from Partisan times.

Le Busette
Castelnuovo, Valsugana
Trento.

13.x.47

The Shelley books and Connolly's arrived just before I left Trieste and I am now reading them with terrific pleasure. I had a slight lapse when I arrived at Trento and had to spend two days in bed – so was very glad not to be in Trieste. It is absolutely lovely here – not a house in sight, the ceaseless noise of running water, a green Alp at our doorstep, huge Dolomiti all around.

We stick to two meals a day – dinner and supper, but drink Grappa – this year's vintage at breakfast. I am now feeling horribly fit – walking a lot and meeting thousands of Victors 'cousins'. We had four to supper last night, polenta and sausages and wine, and they sang the strange songs for hours, which are beautiful.

I enclose also a cutting from the 'Corriere Tridentino' of Oct 11th. It is a short account of a 'gathering' which was held by ANPI, 'The National Association of Italian Partisans', "in my honour". It really was a terrific evening and I made a terrible speech in reply to a welcome from Sig. Ferrandi but it seemed to go down all right. Everyone in fact has been most friendly and I have met many old friends in Rovereto, Milano, (where we spent two nights) and Trento.

Yesterday we went right up the mountains to Castel Tesino where a new Oratorio was being opened. I enclose a postcard memento. It is a rather touching story: The inhabitants swore, on the night of 8 Oct '44, just before the beginning of a terrible rastrellamento (German drive through for Partisans) that if their village was not burnt they would erect a great oratorio in honour of the Madonna. For a small mountain village it is really a very handsome and large building as you can see, and as it was in the area of the Gramschi Brigade, of Nino Nanetti Div, I was glad to be there.

The proceedings were slightly spoiled by a fat and torrid Monsignor who bubbled militantly for far too long; but all the babies howled while he was speaking and I took this to be a good sign.

Today we are going to Asolo (Browning's Villa where Victors brother lives.) Tomorrow meeting Miss Freya Stark (Valley of the Assassins etc) and then to Venice for two days for another partisan celebration. No more now. Next letter to Trieste please. I shall write on the 142nd anniversary.[1]

British Element Trieste Force
Office of the G. O. C.-in-C. (sharp minor)
30.xj.47

Carissima (Italian for Dear Mummy)

As soon as I decided to return to Trieste – the Greek meeting Greek having proved a failure – I found Headquarters had been reorganised (at least, that's the official word: David will give you a more exact interpretation – for there are spies everywhere!!) and I myself transferred or translated from one of the more, to one of the *most*, useless departments. Since then I have been assiduous in creating a suitably chaotic air about the place – which is why I haven't written.

But I *have* dispatched a ham and a lovely box (I hope) of crystalized fruits – and may they bless and grace the Christmas feast. They should arrive I think by the 8th or 10th Dec.

It is most peculiar, but coming back from a longish absence I am even more deferred and referred to than previously. All sorts of Majors whom I don't know call me 'Richard' and ask me to drink and dine. I think they think I'm reporting privately to the Labour Party – I'm the only officer in Trieste – as far as can be ascertained – who voted for them. As each disaster falls, I magnify the virtues of the Government, but at the same time denigrate and vilify the characters of the divers ministers and prominent politicians. This causes a furrore because everybody else vilifies the Government and proclaims that so and so is not a bad chap personally but ...! However, I have no illusions and am preparing to migrate, if necessary to the 1st Battalion where John Freeland is now 2nd ic.

A man is coming to dinner on Tuesday to offer me a chance of serving (I'm being perfectly serious) in the Peruvian army as a parachute King. I shan't tell him I've only done 5 jumps in my life. If the pay is good and I can go, I shall go. If not, not.

The Shelley books are delightful, already I am an authority on the subject. I spent four days at S. Terenzo on the Golfo di Spezia. The Casa Magni (his last home) is now taken by a Monsieur Giorgio (Georges) Popoff, Vice-Consulo di Francia – a very nice young man. His parents were first terrorised and then executed in the Revolution. He emigrated, at the early age of 5 months to Paris and is now naturalised.

In Milan I stayed with Tom Rowarth, who took us to the picture gallery in Venezia. I was amazed – though not really amazed, by his manner of living. As you know he has an operatic wife (very charming) but he also has a Tintoretto, two Guardis, a Canaletto, and various other works of art hung in his rooms.

Where *does* he get them? How does he pay for them? Seedy, silent, men trooped in and out all day, and I can only think he's on a very peculiar, black market etc business.

We heard a very fine concert at La Scala – a Magnificent Theatre. I am entirely in agreement about Aunt Ks present and very sorry to hear of Mickies [2] death. But I think he had a good life and gave great joy, so dying doesn't matter. I think we are inclined to be a little selfish about death. But I do deplore the despair of Mr Winant [3] – what a great man! I think H Truman and Co are directly responsible for his death and would like to arraign them before one of their own blatantly fascist tribunals. One American paper made a joke about poor W.

I hope to stay with the Sonino-Toscolo's at Xmas in Venezia but nothing is certain. They may make me duty officer of Xmas Day.


Jan 4<sup>th</sup> 1948        [Trieste]


I must recall, in order, the so numerous parcels which have arrived; and for all of which very many thanks. Four or five days before Christmas arrived your lovely book parcel. I think the Percy Scholes volumes are magnificent a terrific and most useful book for reference, or before attending the Opera or listening to the radio.

We are now completely on the rocks. The £ sterling is worth only 1,640 lire, and until 31<sup>st</sup> Dec it was at 2,340. So I don't know when I can 'go abroad' to Venezia again. I missed going at

Christmas as I was on duty – not being courageous enough to put anyone else on. Last night we listened to Clement Attlee on his birthday. It began off like a declaration of War on Russia and ended as a party diatribe. What can one think? I have almost decided on the philosophy of heroic vitalism.

I hope to come home on an Air Liaison officers course at Old Sarum about the end of March. This will depend on official consent – but I hope it will be all right. Dicky Johnsen (you will remember in Venice) threatens to visit me in early March on his way to Africa which will be very nice.

Contrary to all expectation this has so far been the mildest winter in almost living memory – only one bora.

5.ii.48      [Trieste]

Many thanks for your last two – 25th and 27th. Glad the fruit arrived almost intact. What possible connection had Joan Easton[4] with the Dragon School. Was it our influence do you think? Poor Bobby I expect he hates the RAOC, but of course the pay is better.

Well the Colonel has promised to procure 'The Strange Life of Ivan' so I hope it will arrive soon. I'm not sure whether its coming here first or not; if it does be assured I will speed it on to you. I think all my books are now arrived but alas not Aunt Ks Chess book.

The other day we saw 'Don Pasquale' at the local opera. Very well done – and on Saturday we are going to 'Mignon' which I am greatly looking forward to. Tomorrow our Mess is throwing a Sherry party, and last Saturday I was up most of the night at the Royal Italian Yacht Club Ball.

Only the Haute Noblesse and ex fascists attended and it was absolutely packed. So you see I lead a debilitatingly gay life!

When it is quieter I play chess in a large café near the Opera House, on the sea front. They have enormous boards and huge chess men – it is great fun. It is a beautiful day. The mountains are out again.

British Element Trieste Force
18.v  [1948?]

Thank you very much for your letter. I may still be able to get the lace, but in any case will get something. I would prefer the lace as it is really remarkably beautiful. If I can raise the ready I will get some glass for a present otherwise shall have to buy a present in England. I'm sure there are still some very nice things.

The situation is this: I have wangled myself on to an eight weeks course which will begin on June 20. I think I shall be home on 18th, try to be anyway. It is a 1st Class course and if I do well it means that, as a Staff Officer, I shall be attached to the RAF. It also means, owing to the length of the course – that I *may* not return to Trieste. However, I'm beginning to feel restless and a change, if it comes, will not be a bad thing. That 'tho is still to be decided. I know Jimmy Lunt will try and get them to agree to my place being kept, but it may not be possible. I shall want my leave after the course, that is certain.

I enclose a mint set of the new Italian stamps celebrating the Risorgimento of 1848. The 100 Lire one represents the Poet Goffredo Manneli on his death bed – he was killed in the siege of Rome 1849.

A beautiful weekend was spent in Venice. It

was a feast – Whitsun, and the Cardinal Patriarch was doing his stuff in San Marco, then there was a monumental display of fireworks on the Canal at night and I spent most of the day on the Laguna.

I have had letters from Joan and David and will certainly be best man but I'm not at all sure – being on this course – that I shall have a lot of time to arrange things. Are we inviting a lot of people? Also I shall have to get a Morning dress (Moss Bros) on hire. I am writing to David to tell him all this. Possibly Jones would fit me out with a suit.


## CHORUS OF THE WOMEN OF POLA
### Enhanced by Ghostly voices – AD 1947.


The Women:

Moon may thy madness
Encompass this City
And no mead of sadness
Resolve the World's pity

For those who are coming
When we are departed -
The lying, the scheming
The ironhearted.

Our city is betrayed
And its virtue lost:
Our dead – true and tried -
Have surrendered at last

Each humble grave
And high borne tomb.
– But their ghosts will grieve
To the end of time

Though they cross the sea
To a land of sorrow,
Where they may be free
Of sleep tomorrow

And evermore;
And they may praise
The sea which mars
But never betrays

The committed dead:
It wraps them round
Caressing each head
Which sleeps so sound

The Women:     World stand appalled:
And damned be they
Who have forestalled
God's Judgement Day.

Voices :     Ah, never again
Will we see the town
Which throbs in the brain
And inhabits the bone.

               – The brain a skull
               The bone a myth -
               The grave a cruel
               Gaping mouth.

               And there's no hope, no love
               No consolation.
               This double death
               This foul oblation

               O cheat, O liar, O Lord,
               Even our dust is designed
               To falsify thy word
               Even the Dead are zoned.

               But Italy, will know us
               When thou Lord art discrowned
               And thy manmade Trinity
               Manhandled and disowned.

**The Women:**    All through the night we have heard
               Coffins being leaded in board
               For the journey beyond the sea -
               And, oh, my dear one your dead hand is cold

**Voices:**          Cold ...

**The Women:**    So far, so far away -
               Are not the dead even, free,
               Malice can go not further
               Than eternity.

                                   **1948**

# THRENODY FOR A FRIEND KILLED IN JERUSALEM[5]

Never again
To know that level place
Which springs with the wind in the wilderness of dawn.
Never again
Watch the long shades unfold and the lonely hills
Echo the day reborn.


Never again
To see the loose -strife weave
A water pattern where the river sweeps.
Never again
To walk at evening westward, where the sun
In unseen glory sleeps.


And now you lie
In a despairing garden: He
Was crucified nearby – but lived again
So there was not much pain.....
But was there any need for you to die?

1947

# 17

## Last Years in the Army

In the summer of 1948, Richard attended a course at RAF West Raynham on Air-Ground cooperation. During this time, his brother David married Joan Easton, Richard acting as Best Man on the occasion. Following the course, Richard was posted as instructor at West Raynham with the Army section. In 1949, he rejoined his Regiment at Aquaba, and also spent some time on the Suez Canal. Back in England in 1950, he attended a Senior Officer's course at Warminster, before returning to the Canal Zone.

Richard's last army years were in the Middle East. Although he always loved his Regiment, he liked the Army less, and some of that feeling appears in the poems.

1st Bn The Royal Sussex Regt
APO 215.MELF.18

Sunday 2 July 1949 [Aquaba]

Many thanks for your three letters (one from Victor), dated 14th, 16th, and 25th June. It appears it was only neccessary to implace the magic 'Par avion' and all is well. I'm sure you will have enjoyed your stay at Harpenden and your visit to Wimbledon. The USA as usual seem to sweep all before them.

I am very busy preparing the Company for the move on July 20th. We had a terrible fire the other day and lost nearly all our band instruments – luckily they are insured to replacement value.

It is about a quarter to eight in the morning now and the Parson is reciting The Nicene Creed in the Church tent next door. Poor man he doesn't get much support 'tho I always go to the 9.15 matins. He is a very worthy but very boring Irishman and has spent most of his time in Military Prisons; consequently his sermons are all admonitory and barked out staccatoesquely, almost angrily: I quite like him.

Must stop now for a shower before breakfast.

9.vj.        [Aquaba]

Just a short line in case there is a plane tomorrow. I will write at length over the week end. We have been envying you your lovely cool weather – only 92 in the shade – and tomorrow we begin 'Summer hours' i.e. we get up even earlier, soon after midnight in fact.

I spent a wonderful day and night in Wadi Rumm yesterday. Our jeep broke down in the desert – I was taking a naval officer on a tour – and we walked miles expecting Hyenas etc. Rumm is marvellous the red sheer cliffs rise 3500 feet out of the valley. Eventually we came to an Arab outpost and spent several hours drinking mint tea and excellent coffee. In the end we got another vehicle, sleeping the night out in the valley – absolutely marvellous – so cool and quiet after Aquaba. Next week I am taking a party to Petra – the rose red city, though my heart goes to Trieste with HMS Chevron – lucky devils!

Chequers is just in. More junketing I expect. I dined and flicked on Chevron on Wednesday, when we had a ceremonial parade for HMs Birthday. I commanded 'A' Company.

## RUDOLF SLANSKY 3 Dec '52[1]

'Rapidissimo e stato il trapasso della poltrona di comando alla forca'.

'Secondo qualcuno, nel carcere di Pancra sono state erette tre forchs per potar procedere piu rapidemente alle execuzioni.'

Do not discount them, who died
Although in another cause
They are on reason's side
Dead servants of her laws.


Oppression opened their eyes
Tyranny threw them in court
Slaves accepted the lies
Which they themselves had taught.


So they were hanged in a row
Martyrs to their own lives
Nobody else in the know –
Only their courage survives

5 December

## "THE EGYPTIANS WHOM YE HAVE SEEN TODAY, YE SHALL SEE THEM AGAIN NO MORE FOR EVER."

Fires gleam on Ataqa and moonlight glows
In mild white particles of brilliance on Suez shore.
Within the bay ships ride on leaden helm ...
The Ghost of Tewfik sighs and takes a train
Private, of course – past Abbas' palace and past
Bleak thoughts of greatness written in his brain.

The King of Egypt sits in his palace and scratches
Until the palace is no longer there.

Sickle, the moon descends on desert wastes
Launching her anarchy upon the silent sand,
And God – who is only one – nods and falls asleep
Beside the cultural fires of western lands;
While barren regions prod a barren king
Fitfully to make commands.

The King looks madly in a looking-glass
And yet the mirror will not look at him.

Beside the level waters Midian waits,
The gypsies take their toll, and millionaires
Rub spineless hand in hand and hazard guesses
Which are confirmed later in the Financial Times
And might have been read in the smile on the face of
the Sphynx

Penniless officers congregate in messes
But the King of Egypt scratches – and understands.

Tewfik wilts, Abbas declines; Fuad raises a head
On coin o' the realm, raises a son and dies.
He, the unsightly one, raises his double chins
And looks towards Mecca with a fond surmise.
A still small voice in diplomatic ffrench
Somewhere enjoins, 'Maison de Jacob venez,
et marchons . . .'

The King of Egypt nearly has a fit,
Recovers  reason and has a  couple of djins.


BALLAD OF EGYPTIAN DARKNESS

Sailing lights somberly
Move shipshape where water lies,
Fades the dove to raven twilight
- Radio Muezzin cries:
Praise be to Allah
Who three worlds made,
Him only we worship,
Seek only his aid.
As for the unbelievers
It matters not:
God has sealed up their hearts
- They've had their lot.
Down in the French town

By the crocodile lake
The faithful, undeparting,
Have eaten, and want more, cake.
Low over the desert
A white wind blows.
French town is done for,
And the desert knows.
Like a beggar waiting
By the edge of despair
Old nomad desert
Sniffs the charnel air
The glories of Misr
Were ruins before
Time ran up these shacks at
Eternity's back-door –

Dawn groans: and misery
Squats in the land.
The accurate sunlight
Spits on the sand.


PRAYER

Lord clasp Egypt to thy breast
Succour us thy poor distressed
Stationed here at least three years
Watering Egypt with our tears.

By the sound of lapping waters-
By the King of Egypt's daughters-

By the COs monthly snorters
Give us despair O Lord.

Lord the weather here is hot
Lord I wish that it was not.
Send me please to cooler climes-
Deliver me the morning 'Times'.

Lord, where the common tongue is wog
I may be pi – I am not dog.
If thy sarvant thou wouldst please
Send him to the Antipodes.

When the Red Sea runs with blood
When the sun is shott with mud
When the sphinx is put to stud
You'll send us Lord to the Sudan
Or even worse to Abadan.


CHECK TO THE KING

Narriman Regina Loquitur:
(allegro ma non troppo)

I and the King in Egypt
Like lovers, hand in hand
Attempted ffrase or two in ffrench
Which lovers understand

(PPP)

I did not lie to him
He wished to lie with me
So in the Abdin palace
We lied agreeably.
(fort)
And now I wear a coronet
In place of maidenhead
– He'll find it damned uncomfortable  (presto)
When next we go to bed.


EYE-WITNESS


Come off it, Judas.  Stop it, do...
Don't do nothing to hurt yourself
Thirty quid and an Empire gong –
Well, if you must... to Hell with you.


Oh, a nine days wonder: not even that
Bald-headed old fool who started it,
Dipping his hands in a prissy way
Though the sentence came out pat:


'Hanged on a cross until you're dead.'
I ask you!  How, in these bloody times
With a dozen gods to pacify,
Can a sane man keep his head?

I'd always thought that one of those,
Jesus or Judas – now both of them's dead –
Would give us a lead: but which betrayed
T'other, if either did, God knows.


## FIRST LET ME TALK WITH THIS PHILOSOPHER


Though I had often heard before
That soldiers swore and diced
By Golgotha, I'd never heard
The 'solar myth' of Christ.


A greater blasphemy; because
The soldiers wouldn't know
What they were doing – soldiers are
Obedient but slow.


But truth is truth – and more than truth
When hammered to a tree –
A 'solar myth' poor symbol of
Man's unreality.


"Lord if he sleep, he shall do well."
No more, perhaps, sufficed
The wretch who called kenotic God
Divine discarnate Christ.

## SYNOD

The synod nodded its holy head,
A bishop murmured a benediction,
A popular minister gave his views
On the concrete benefits of conscription.

'The young' he said, 'will get tougher and tougher
'And H.M.G. can bluff bluffer and bluffer;
'The Church's conscience, of course, will suffer –
'Rough on the Church – but it could be rougher.'

Great the applause which greeted this
Totalitarian concept of bliss.
A Dean or two were heard to hiss
Gloomy remarks on atomic fiss-

Ion, and the minor role assigned
To the wondrous all-creating mind.
'God's in his heaven and his hell'
Vouchsafed the Bishop, 'so all is well'.


## IN PIAM MEMORIAM IOHANNI FLEETWOOD: OBIIT MCMLIV[2]

No epitaph occurs to me.
His mind at rest
In a tomb cradled by the nursery sea
Whose homely looks compel no interest,
Whose ripples wake their own monotony.

The sly land sidles to the sea
Wade tideless here,
Where sea and land merge imperceptibly
Within a mind whose mortal riches were
Conferred by world-revealing ecstacy


Beyond awareness of the day
When he should cease.
Breath mocks the past and time recalls his clay,
Whose youth refashioned kingdoms to release
A spirit that no wisdom could betray.

## Post-script Italian Poems

Most of these poems were written in the year after Richard left the army. He spent much of 1953 at Le Busette, Victor Gozzer's house in the Val Sugana. Much later he wrote the poem about Tom Rowarth. He had known him in SOE with the partisans, and refers to him rather unflatteringly in his war diary. And yet.... this was in fact the last poem he wrote, in 1984, returning to those Partisan days which had meant so much to him.


## ITALIA

"Libertà non tradisce i volenti"

Embodiment of dreams and all desires
- Vicegerent of the sun – in unquiet darkness
Outpacing all the ages;
When tonight thy spirit soars,
Under its pale aegis
I would away
On heaven's eternal tide
To wander wakingly
Over the waters wide
Which cleave me from a magic land,
Cherished in my imagining
-Unhappy now and sorrowing –
Which yet enchains my mind,

When the strait evening wind
Jostles the leaves, and trees

Are silhouette, and soft moon ladders
Reach silently to earth, I will ascend
On these and come with you
And travel over sea and land
In everlasting night the whole world through.
And men may say
- Seeing the glorious windspun stars
Stand out so bright
And knowing not what pity stirs -
'There is a languid moon tonight
Almost she faints for loss of light.'

So we will come to Italy
– White cradle of the mind, enslaved
Still;- by eternal tideless waters laved,
The ancient home of liberty;
Mother and heir of Leopardi's sorrow;
We feel the sadness of her genius now
Ponder the secret stirring of tomorrow.
Saddest heart
In a world esteemed sad
With all her glories as dim banners furled.

Ills have increased their fears
Who are below. Only from time to time
We see the gemlike fires
Which signal freedom – not yet in the tomb.
Men live while they draw breath
And have not failed
Because they have not felt
That subtil disillusion which is death.

Comrades, your lives are set
Within the hills which are God's monument
In this fair land. As we advance
And our pale glance falls on the northern bastion
The Alps, now I, insatiate
Of other times, know shadows immanent
Keen cut and clear, their snowy island peaks
O'ertop the silvered and serene
Lagoon of cloud.
The wind, our escort, echoes loud
Old memories through the forest green
Betrayed passes.

I had walked
Only a year ago these silent hills.
Seen Venice and the Veneto when the sun waked
Our patriots with a bloodred urgent hail
Over the Adriatic.  Blood was god.
In those red days, the fighting was most good.
For us, alas, the mood
Is gone or buried with our friends
In unknown graves.  The whole world grieves;
We who are left should make amends.

   Brief is our stay
   And I must say farewell
To you who are my waking and my sleeping
First thoughts; and through each day
I only think of you; and when I die
I shall be with you on the day of weeping.

# A BALLAD OF LAKE GARDA

It's Garda – and Germans! in springtime the sun
Alights on the lake and the skin of the Hun
Spreadeagled like swastikas, flat on their backs –
With singular women in angular slacks.

And the rubicund ghost of Radetsky in wine
Surveys, with impatience, these Gadarene swine;
With an angry, prospective an ownery look
He consignes to the devil the handmaid of Cook.

"O Gardasee, Gardasee! Gnadige Frau
The lake is so German as you must allow
The Forland – though Alpen – sweeps down to the
      lake ...
Francesco-Guiseppe was such a mistake

With his weakness and petulance – fifty long years
Of bureaucracy; weakened his hold on the tears
Of Venetian and Lombard: Vittorio E
Put nails in the coffin of OUR Gardasee".

But the angular women in Singular slacks
And the he-men with bellies which bulge through
      their backs
Will dream in the sun and expand in the see
'Till it brims and runs over in High Germanee.

## VALSUGANA

Mountains are getting nervous, snow is in the air
Clouds, uncertain, huddle on the windy stair.
Summer and regret are gone.

Snow is down to earth here; we are on the wrong
Side of the sun – shadow, immanent all day long,
Snow and Grappa remain.

Sun is whiter than the snow, and the sleighting snow
Does a disappearing trick; we are in the know;
Landscape and warmth appear.

Not for very long, though; whiteness on the night –
Noiseless; no moon, no stars, and, muffled up tight,
Snow and cold are here.


## LE BUSETTE

Outside the night; within the moon
Concentrates this little room.

Gentle light conceals the place
From its ordinary grace

Most fantastic shadows peer
From the mountains which are near,

While the moving water fills
Thoughts with Spring upon the hills

But the winter cold is nigh
And the winds perpetual sigh

About the house reveals the snow
Cringing in the mountains now,

Waiting till a whiter morn
Cries in labour : winter born.

But now the lamps are lit, and I
Will not see the autumn die.

## TORCELLO

That seaward sound again... the idle night
Is tossing stars deep into the lagoon:
Light still enshrines an altar in the West.

This tower in silence rests upon the night
And, like a sign-post studied long, assists
Quietly the patterned shadow of a moon.

High on these ancient stones beyond, the night
A future victim shoulders destiny:
Sightless, accepts the darkness he resists
And sets his thoughts beyond the pale of night.

## THE LAST LIGHT

Within the shattered bowl
A last light gleams.
The ultimate music schemes
On frisky strings – all makes for sadness
And my last window on the world is shuttered.

I am confused by Raffaello,
Michelangelo confounds me
When I remember the pale gold look
Of my lover beyond the sea.

His beauty is painted by them
But they never knew him
Can he live in their memory
Long after they are dead?

Guided by mountains he persists
In discontent far, far away.
And I may never go to him
Nor will he ever come to me.


## MUZTAGH ATA
### H.W.T.

Lord Tilman exalted mountains.
Considered, and climbed 'em

He climbed hours and concentrated metres
Within his boots

He measured beauty
By difficulty.

He considered necessity
Unnecessary.

He called the source of a river
Its impenetrability.

Skill was a condition
Some failed to keep.

Misery a measure
Of indecision.

Where the world joins
He set his tent

And recommended Atlas
To heave the sky higher.

-Rakoposhi was
A dispensation to Gods

Everest a yearning
Higher than despair -

Despair an elation

## TOM ROWARTH'S GRAVE

Rowarth Thomas Ivan
Rotherham.............I.
Strange, did you wish
To be known in death
By such a name as this?
Place name of your infancy,
Ignominy, grief perhaps
So that when life itself
Shipwrecked on beautiful shores
Gave up its breath
You thought
Yorkshire I was and am:
By this Italian shore
I was, I am.

# Epilogue

I have enjoyed reading Richard's letters and poems and putting this volume together, and I have learned a lot about army life. Reading the letters, I was amazed that in the middle of the war, when he kept moving from one place to another, he seemed to receive so many letters. Even when he was behind enemy lines, letters and books came in by parachute. Amid the chaos of war, someone must have been doing something right. And so many of the letters he wrote found their way safely back to England.

In the early years, much time seems to have been devoted to sport – even when France was being invaded, they were playing cricket on the fields of Picardie. Perhaps this was what he thought his mother would be most interested to hear about. I was also struck by the fact that you could go looking for a job, you hadn't got to rely on just being sent. Promotion came and went – apparently according to vacancies in the higher rank. The addition or loss of a pip was an important matter. Of course it is also clear how times have changed.

Throughout his army career, Richard was always searching for an interesting posting. He also found a very interesting job in his civilian career.

After he left the Army, Richard went to Italy where he spent nearly a year, 1953, staying mainly in Victor Gozzer's house, Le Busette, in the Val Sugana. There he wrote a little, and nourished his love of Italy, its language, its people, its music, its history. In 1954, he became Private Secretary and ADC to the Governor of the Leeward Islands, Sir Kenneth Blackburn, and was based in Antigua. He and I were married there in 1955.

On returning to England, Richard taught for a short time at A.S.Neill's school, Summerhill, the most "progressive" of all the progressive schools. He named A.S.Neill, and the Colonel of his Regiment, Brigadier Foster, as his two referees when he applied to become a Probation Officer. Neill described Richard as " A gentleman in the best sense, a scholar, very human, never the moraliser or judger ".

Richard joined the London Probation service in 1960, which led him in due course to the Court Welfare Department. He joined the team at the Royal Courts of Justice, and ended his career there as Senior Court Welfare Officer.  He retired, reluctantly, on his 65th birthday in 1984.

We moved to Oxford in 1988, where Richard spent the rest of his life, enjoying the bookshops, the music and the beauty of that city whose last enchantments can still occasionally be experienced. In 1997, on a return visit to Italy, he was made a "Cittadinanza Honoraria" of the town Vittorio Veneto, in recognition of his wartime contribution. He died on June 10th, 2006.

Richard kept all the letters he ever received.  Among them was one from Sir Kenneth Blackburn, which said "it was wonderful to have such an equable person living in the house."  I received many letters from his colleagues at the Law Courts after he died.

Here are some of the things they wrote:

*I first met him at the Royal Courts of Justice where he steadily and quietly built a happy ship at the High Court. He was always ready with an apt quote from the classics and under his influence we share still his eloquent contempt for cant and hypocrisy.*

*Although I have not seen Richard for some time, I retain a grateful memory of all his wisdom, and kindness to me.  In his essentially individual way, he was a super Senior Court Welfare Officer much respected by all who knew him.*

*I was so privileged to have Richard as my first Senior when I became a welfare officer at the Royal Courts.*

*Working with such a fine scholar and gentleman was a very rewarding experience.*

*I had seven happy years at the Royal Courts of Justice with Richard and our other colleagues. It was a wonderful team under Richard's guidance.*

Richard was a modest man. I hope, but I am not completely sure, that he would be pleased with what I have done. I am certain, however, that he would know it was done with love.

# Notes

## Chapter 1

1  Barossa – a heathland near Sandhurst
2  The Palace – the house of the Commanding Officer
3  Sir Thomas Inskip, Minister for co-ordination of Defence, 1936 -1939. This was a controversial appointment, as Churchill had been expected to get the job. The jibe was made: "This is the most cynical appointment since Caligula made his horse a Consul."
4  The Shop – refers to the Royal Military Academy, Woolwich, where military engineers, or "Sappers", trained

## Chapter 2

1.  Alice Delysia – French singer and actress, 1889-1979, popular in London in 1920s – 30s
2.  Old Contemptibles- name given to soldiers of the British Expeditionary Force who held the line in the first battle of Ypres, on or before November 22nd 1914. The Kaiser had described them as a "contemptible little Army"
3.  April crisis- probably refers to further threats against Poland
4.  The Military Training Act of April 1939 conscripted men aged 20 – 21 . In October it was extended to men between 18 and 41, except for those in reserve occupations.
5  35th – 35th Regiment of Foot, The Royal Sussex
6  Roussillon Gazette – the Regimental Magazine
7  The Depot – at Chichester, where the Royal Sussex Regiment was based

## Chapter 4

1  Mussolini had let it be known that Italy would enter the war on the side of Germany
2  Germany invaded Belgium and Holland on May 10th
3  King Leopold III surrendered unconditionally to the German army, against the wishes of most of his people. At the time he was regarded as a traitor.

4 Many men of the 2nd Battalion were taken prisoner at Dunkirk and remained prisoners of war until 1945

5 Italy declared war on France and Britain on June 10th

Chapter 6

1. Quags – Quaglino's, a well known London restaurant.

2. Sir Samuel Hoare – one time Member of Parliament for Chelsea, as Foreign Secretary signed the Hoare – Laval pact with France in 1935 giving legitimacy to Mussolini's invasion of Abyssinia. Churchill sent him to Madrid as ambassador in 1940. Laval was a member of the Vichy Government which had negotiated with Germany.

3 Audrey Lynam – daughter of the Dragon School headmaster

4 A modest attempt at secrecy

5 Tubby – a master at the Dragon School

6 Uncle B – General Sir Bernard Paget – see page 10

7 The routing of Mountcalm at Quebec by General Woolf was a famous Royal Sussex victory – September 13th 1759

8 Eve of Waterloo – June 17th 1815

9. Funeral of Brigadier Richard Maule Birkett, Colonel of the Royal Sussex Regiment 1941 – 42

Chapter 7

1 Paget – see page 10

Chapter 8

1 Halton – the Tolson family house in Harpenden was taken over by King Peter of Yugoslavia

2 Trafalgar Day was always remembered by Richard and his Mother – October 21st

3 The French "up the road" refers to Lebanon

4 See note one – obviously some problems there

Chapter 9

1. March 17th was the anniversary of the death of Richard's brother John.

Chapter 10
1. Uncle B – see page 10
2. April 12th – anniversary of the death of Richard's father.
3. Punch, a dog, and Judith (I think) a hen

Chapter 11
1. "How right you were" – Richard's mother had tried to dissuade him from going in to the army.
2. Bastille day in France – a celebration of the Revolution.

Chapter 12
1. Piave – all the Partisans had war names – *nomme di Guerra* – as will be apparent throughout the diary.
2. Rastrellamento – literally "raking through" – in fact a German attack
3. Trafalgar day – note [2] chapter 8
4. The Major – Major Tilman, a famous mountaineer and adventurer, and an inspirational leader.
5. Vittorio – Vittorio Gozzer, known as Tito or Victor, a lifelong friend of Richard's. He and his family lived in Milan and the Val Sugana.
6. Norman – Norman Paley Norton from South Africa, also a good friend
7. January 11th rastrallamento – this was the biggest set-back they had during Richard's time with the Partisans
8. Nello – Lanfranco Canniato, from Venice, joined aged 17, and he and his English wife Alison also became lifelong friends

Chapter 13
1. Nora – Richard's contact in England, who kept in touch with his mother.

Chapter 14
1. Palmer and Frank Thompson – friends from the Dragon School. Frank was also in SOE but was killed in Eastern Europe

2.   Bertram – I think refers to the cat

Chapter 16
1.   Trafalgar Day – again
2.   Mickie – a Maltese Terrier, winner of many prizes
3.   John Gilbert  Winant – was United States Ambassador to
     the U.K.from  1941 to  1946.  He was a great Anglophile.
     He was appointed to a United Nations position after the
     war, but was replaced by Averill Harriman, and soon after
     committed suicide.

4.   Joan Easton married David Tolson on August 7th 1948.  She
     was briefly a Matron at the Dragon School.  Her brother
     Hugh was known as Bobby.
5.   George Dickie Clarke, killed in Jerusalem 1946

Chapter 17
1.   Rudolf Slansky was a Czeckoslovakian Communist leader,
     much in favour with Russia during and after the war.
     However, he lost approval in 1951, and confessed under
     torture to spying for the West.  He was sentenced to death,
     and was executed on December 3rd 1952.
2.   Johnny Fleetwood was killed in Italy in October 1944
     while serving with the Royal Hampshire Regiment. He was
     originally with the Royal Sussex, and he is mentioned in a
     letter of July 1943 . His  name appears with those of several
     other friends who were killed in the fly-leaf of Richard's  copy
     of the  works of William Blake, mentioned on page 167.

# Glossary

| | |
|---|---|
| ARP | Air Raid Precautions |
| BEF | British Expeditionary Force |
| BHQ | Battalion Headquarters |
| BLO | British Liaison Officer |
| BT (SIAM) | British Troops (SIAM) |
| CMF | Central Mediterranean Forces |
| CO | Commanding Officer |
| CSM | Company Sergeant Major |
| DCM | Distinguished Service Medal |
| DO | Demi – Official |
| DZ | Dropping Zone |
| FANY | First Aid Nursing Yeomanry |
| GC | Gentleman Cadet |
| GC | George Cross |
| GHQ | General Headquarters |
| G1 | General Staff Officer Grade 1 |
| GOC | General Officer Commanding |
| HMG | Heavy Machine Gun |
| HQ | Headquarters |
| ITC | Infantry Training Centre |
| ITD | International Transit Depot |
| JT & FSR | Joint Training & Field Service Regulations |
| ME | Middle East |
| MEF | Middle East Forces |
| MO | Medical Officer |
| MG | Machine Gun |
| NCO | Non Commissioned Officer |
| O&A | Organisation and Administration |

| | |
|---|---|
| OB | Old Brightonian (Pupil of Brighton College) |
| OD | Old Dragon (Pupil of the Dragon School) |
| POW | Prisoner of War |
| PRI | President of Regimental Institute (provides funding for Extras such as sports equipment) |
| PW | Psychological Warfare |
| QM | Quarter Master |
| RAMC | Royal Army Medical Corps |
| RARO | Regular Army Reserve of Officers |
| RASC | Royal Army Service Corps |
| RMC | Royal Military College (Sandhurst) |
| RSM | Regimental Sergeant Major |
| RTC | Royal Tank Corps |
| SEAC | South East Asia Command |
| SLI | Somerset Light Infantry |
| SR – SRO | Supplementary Reserve – Supplementary Reserve of Officers |
| TA | Territorial Army |
| TEWT | Tactical Exercise Without Troops |

# INDEX